The Calling: Releasing Christians Into their Full Potential

Chris A. Legebow

ISBN: 978-1-988914-14-5

DEDICATION

This book is dedicated to those who taught me Bible classes, Minister's Candidate school as well as Minister's Training School. Also, I thank the ministries that have impacted my life for Spiritual growth as a Christian.

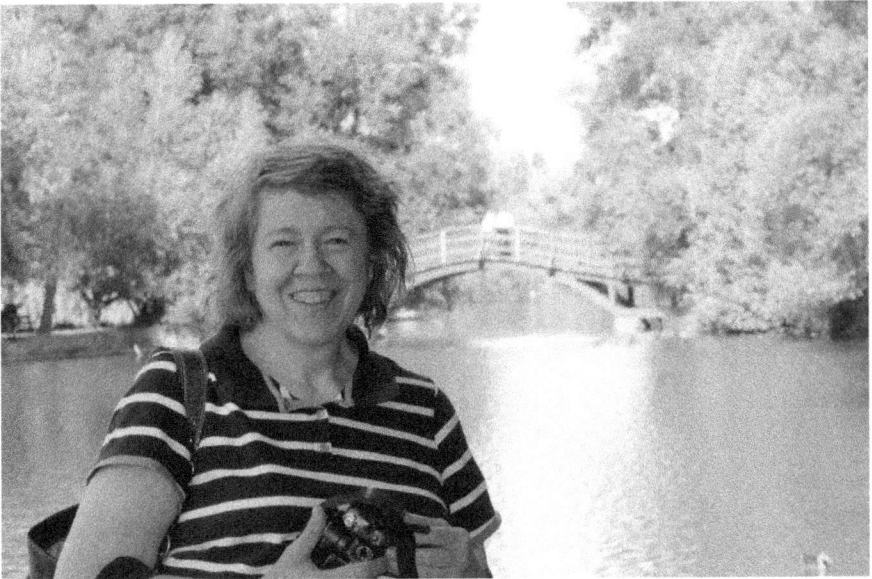

CONTENTS

ACKNOWLEDGMENTS

Bible Gateway .com KJV, NIV, MEV, NLT

1 INTRODUCTION

You are interested in becoming more than an average Christian or you wouldn't be reading this book. This book is for those who want to yield their lives, so that Christ can use them. It is a book of radical Christian devotion – not religion. It is devotion to Christ. The book discusses three main phases of ministry or calling. By ministry I mean Christian Church, but I also mean letting God use you through your secular career so that you can shine for Christ. I emphasize all Christians are called into the ministry – some in the Church always, some in the Career but also the Church. It starts with prayer. Pray that God would release labourers into the earth. Pray that you yourself can be a labourer.

Prepare yourself with education, experience etc. Mentorship is essential to your growth. There should be people speaking into your life to cause you to use your gifts and talents. Pray for a mentor and recognize the mentor once he or she arrives in your life. Get all the education, experience, service you can by pursuing Christ first always. Train others as soon as you can. Sow into others lives becoming a mentor to others. Realize your investment in others is essential. You are a part of the Body of Christ. The parts must build up, encourage, enrich each other . Leaders should be training other leaders. Yes, it is essential that you reproduce yourself by training others to live to their full potential.

Section 1

Matthew 9: [35]And Jesus went about all the cities and villages, teaching in their synagogues, and preaching the gospel of the kingdom, and healing every sickness and every disease among the people.

[36]But when he saw the multitudes, he was moved with compassion on them, because they fainted, and were scattered abroad, as sheep having no shepherd.

[37]Then saith he unto his disciples, The harvest truly is plenteous, but the labourers are few;

[38]Pray ye therefore the Lord of the harvest, that he will send forth labourers into his harvest.

Jesus was followed by multitudes. He had compassion on them because they had no shepherd. He fed the 5,000 because he was moved with compassion. His prayer request was prayer for labourers. He ministered to thousands, but more disciples would mean more people could be healed, delivered, or receive the good news of Jesus. You're agreement to live for Christ is your answer to Jesus' prayer. You yield your life to Christ but also train others. Should each person impact his or her sphere of authority, millions of Christians will rise to excellence.

Jesus had 12 disciples. He could use hundreds of them, thousands of them. He saw the crowds of thousands but he also knew of the millions of people who would be birthed on the earth and knew that the only way the gospel could reach the whole world is that hundreds of thousands, millions of disciples, Christ followers would be necessary. His prayer for labourers was a prayer for the rest of human history not simply for the duration of his life. His life sacrifice was not only for those who lived on the earth during his life but for all humans that existed since Adam and Eve, also all who would come after him until the end of the earth or earth age.

After his resurrection

In Mark 16. he told his disciples to preach the gospel to all people, nations - signs and wonders following the preached Word. He anointed them with authority to do it. The same commission applies to all Christians. We are to preach, teach, Christ to the nations – making disciples until Christ returns. Jesus commanded it. He also gave us the authority to do it. Both are necessary. The empowering presence of the Holy Spirit with the Baptism of the Holy Spirit gave the disciples boldness to preach Christ in all of Israel and parts of Europe and Christianity continued to spread throughout the earth.

Mark 16: [15]And he said unto them, Go ye into all the world, and preach the gospel to every creature.

[16]He that believeth and is baptized shall be saved; but he that believeth not shall be damned.

[17]And these signs shall follow them that believe; In my name shall they cast out devils; they shall speak with new tongues;

[18]They shall take up serpents; and if they drink any deadly thing, it shall not hurt them; they shall lay hands on the sick, and they shall recover.

[19] So then after the Lord had spoken unto them, he was received up into heaven, and sat on the right hand of God.

[20] And they went forth, and preached every where, the Lord working with them, and confirming the word with signs following. Amen.

Jesus' promise of following the preaching of the Word with signs and wonders made their gospel more than words to the crowds that heard them. It is the same Holy Spirit that dwells in us that gives us the authority and the unction to preach Christ. The "power" is the gifts of the Spirit along with the fruit of the Spirit. The fruit of the Spirit allows to exemplify Christ and live a godly life. The gifts of the Spirit enable us to effectively minister in the supernatural.

Acts 1: [8] But ye shall receive power, after that the Holy Ghost is come upon you: and ye shall be witnesses unto me both in Jerusalem, and in all Judaea, and in Samaria, and unto the uttermost part of the earth.

The book of Acts is filled with the miracles of the disciples who preached and taught Jesus with miracles following the preached word. It began the start of the Church Age. Before it was the covenant of Moses. We are living in the Church Age and shall continue to do so until the end of the earth. The Church is God's witness of Christ on the earth. Because the Holy Spirit dwells in believers, we are the Body of Christ on the earth. Each member of the body of Christ is important.

1 Corinthians 12: [27] Now ye are the body of Christ, and members in particular.

An example of the ministry of the Apostles is when Peter and John were on their way to prayer meeting. Both of them were doing ordinary but important Christian life things such as going to a prayer meeting. In the midst of their ordinary lives, came a situation of someone who was lame from birth. He cried out begging because he had no other way to live. He wanted money because he didn't know there was any other answer. Peter and John had treasure within them in the Holy Spirit. They did not simply give him money. They spoke life into him that caused his life to radically change.

Acts 3:1 Now Peter and John went up together into the temple at the hour of prayer, being the ninth hour.

[2] And a certain man lame from his mother's womb was carried, whom they laid daily at the gate of the temple which is called Beautiful, to ask alms of them that entered into the temple;

[3] Who seeing Peter and John about to go into the temple asked an alms.

[4] And Peter, fastening his eyes upon him with John, said, Look on us.

[5] And he gave heed unto them, expecting to receive something of them.

The lame man was expecting to receive either silver or gold. He received something beyond what could have naturally occurred. Peter spoke the Word of healing to him by saying "In the name of Jesus Christ of Nazareth, rise up and walk". What occurred is Peter grasped his arm and the lame man obeyed in faith. He stood, immediately strength was in his body. He could walk, run, leap. He was no longer lame. He could use his life to share what Jesus had done for him. It was the faith of the Apostles in Jesus Christ and the authority of his word to preach the good news. The good news for that lame man was he was healed and could now enjoy his life as other people. Now he could speak of what Jesus had done for him through Peter and John. The authority of Jesus was invoked by their faith in Jesus name.

Acts 3: 6 Then Peter said, Silver and gold have I none; but such as I have give I thee: In the name of Jesus Christ of Nazareth rise up and walk.

7 And he took him by the right hand, and lifted him up: and immediately his feet and ankle bones received strength.

8 And he leaping up stood, and walked, and entered with them into the temple, walking, and leaping, and praising God.

The Book of Acts is full of examples of miracles, salvations, healings and deliverance. The Apostles obeyed God. There were 120 of them gathered in the upper room who received the Baptism of the Holy Spirit as Jesus promised. But they were so empowered by the presence of the Baptism of the Holy Spirit or immersion in the Holy Spirit by Jesus, they were compelled to go into the streets of Jerusalem praising God, worshipping God and witnessing of the glory of God. The disciples were speaking and worshipping in tongues and some people questioned it as though the men were drunk. Others who were from other nations received words of encouragement in the languages of their country. God supernaturally gave the disciples the gift of speaking in tongues. Some of them were speaking in languages of the earth they had never studied. Peter answered those who were questioning them as though they were drunken. Peter was anointed by God to speak.

Acts 2: ¹⁵For these are not drunken, as ye suppose, seeing it is but the third hour of the day.

¹⁶But this is that which was spoken by the prophet Joel;

¹⁷And it shall come to pass in the last days, saith God, I will pour out of my Spirit upon all flesh: and your sons and your daughters shall prophesy, and your young men shall see visions, and your old men shall dream dreams:

¹⁸And on my servants and on my hand maidens I will pour out in those days of my Spirit; and they shall prophesy:

¹⁹And I will shew wonders in heaven above, and signs in the earth beneath; blood, and fire, and vapour of smoke:

²⁰The sun shall be turned into darkness, and the moon into blood, before the great and notable day of the Lord come:

²¹And it shall come to pass, that whosoever shall call on the name of the Lord shall be saved.

There is no cancellation of the gifts of the Spirit. The gifts of the Spirit are for the Church. The thousands who gathered that day were pricked in their hearts by Peter's preaching. They believed Jesus Christ was Messiah. They asked how they could be saved. Peter answered them. The gifts of the Spirit were for them and all that came after them as many as received Christ.

Acts 2: **38** Then Peter said unto them, Repent, and be baptized every one of you in the name of Jesus Christ for the remission of sins, and ye shall receive the gift of the Holy Ghost.

39 For the promise is unto you, and to your children, and to all that are afar off, even as many as the LORD our God shall call.

The Church grew exponentially. Those who received Jesus were baptized and filled with the Holy Ghost. Acts 1: **41** Then they that gladly received his word were baptized: and the same day there were added unto them about three thousand souls.

Many of the Christians were from other countries bringing the gospel back to their countries. The Holy Spirit gave the disciples boldness, accuracy, authority to preach the gospel with signs and wonders following the preaching.

The history of the Church was one of multiplication, glory, excitement. But Israel was occupied by Rome. There was persecution from The Pharisees and Sadducees (Religious Jews) and by Rome. Many Christians were martyred for their faith. All of the disciples were martyred except John who survived being boiled in oil. He was sentenced to live on Patmos a deserted Island filled with snakes. Christianity really spread once one of the Roman Emperor's became a Christian. Constantine declaration of Christianity made it safe for Christians. Christianity spread throughout Europe and throughout the Roman Empire. Because Latin was the main language – all of the countries could receive the gospel. The First Bible printed was in Latin. Even though the majority of the free world gets the scriptures in their language and can freely worship God, many people do not know Christ. In other

countries not free, Christians are killed or jailed or abused for their
faith.

Those who founded North America came bringing Christianity
as a primary reason for coming, obeying the commission. Many
Christians who were baptized in the Holy Spirit or who strictly
adhered to the scriptures were persecuted in Europe after the
Protestant Church arose. Christians who wanted freedom of
expression, freedom of worship came to the United States of
America – Christians came to Canada. For the same reasons –
bringing the gospel. Of course. there were people who were with
wrong motive that abused the Native people of North America.
There were many of them. The abuse of the Native North
Americans is with no excuse or pardon – forgiveness only in the
blood of Jesus. The truth is though that Christianity became
predominant in North America. Many of our laws were based on
Leviticus. Much of our government was shaped by the truths of
Scripture.

Until the 1950's we were known as a Christian people. There
was a great revival in the late 1940's. The gifts of the Spirit were
quickened in the Church mightily. Although the majority of the
people still claimed to be Christians, in the 1960's, many people
began a "looser" Bible not adhering to the Scriptures. In the
1970"s a glorious thing occurred in the USA and parts of Canada –
a fresh Charismatic revival – the gifts of the Spirit in not only the
Protestant churches but in the Catholic Church. There have been
waves of God's glory constantly released as people gathered
together to pray, worship study scripture. The purpose of this book
is not to discuss in detail all of the history of the Charismatic
Church but it is well worth reading. I mention that the Charismatic

Church or the Church believing in the gifts of the Spirit has existed since the book of Acts, and has always had a remnant of believers on the earth. There are millions of Charismatic Christians on the earth. There are so many different denominations. but the main beliefs are the same. The Scriptures are God's Word. The gifts of the Spirit are for today. The commission is essential.

Main denominations are Assemblies of God, Pentecostal Assemblies of Canada, Four square Church, Full Gospel Church, Word of Faith, Word of Life churches, Charismatic Independent Churches etc. Should all the believing Charismatic Christians pray for revival, we would receive a world wide revival as has never yet been. I am believing for it. There are thousands of Christians who are believing God for revival. Revival means bringing God's Scriptures as inerrant truth. It means living a holy life, morally, sexually pure. It means the word of God is in our hearts and lives not simply a belief but a lifestyle. It means Christians are making disciples. It means Christians are evangelizing, serving, giving, ministering, praying.

2 Chronicles 7: [14] If my people, which are called by my name, shall humble themselves, and pray, and seek my face, and turn from their wicked ways; then will I hear from heaven, and will forgive their sin, and will heal their land.

There are of course hundreds of thousands if not millions of Christians who are living in revival – but the prayer is that all who are Christians would live what we proclaim we believe. Keeping in communion with Christ, honouring God's Word, doing the works of Christ on the earth, preaching, teaching, healing, delivering etc. is the passion of those living in the Spirit – with God. The desire is that we can glorify Christ with our lives and we can bring the gospel of Jesus Christ to all people on the earth.

Joel 2: [28] And it shall come to pass afterward, that I will pour out my spirit upon all flesh; and your sons and your daughters shall prophesy, your old men shall dream dreams, your young men shall see visions:

[29] And also upon the servants and upon the handmaids in those days will I pour out my spirit.

1. What was the main interest that attracted you to this book? How does it relate to your life?

2. Explain your desire for ministry in the Church? What capacity are you serving in now? What would you desire to do in the Church?

3. What is your career goal? Explain what must occur in as many points as necessary so you may obtain your career goal.

2 EVANGELISM

Most people who live in Western Society get some chance to hear the gospel of Jesus Christ through media or family or friends. Yet there are thousands of people in North America who do not know the truth of Jesus only sort of cute or interesting stories about him. The truth of His sacrifice as God's Son, without sin, humbled by being a human baby, living an earthly life as other humans, dying for our sins so we can be saved, should we but believe in him, doesn't always get preached. It is the essential gospel. Our own communities are mission fields for Christians to share Christ in. Whatever your personal interests are, sports, music, theatre, technology etc. The gospel message get there. In your career, you may be the only Christian someone there has ever met. Your life as a witness for Christ is necessary.

Most common evangelism is one on one. It is how Jesus ministered to the woman at the well in Samaria (John 4: 7-27). It is God using someone's spiritual gifts and talents to speak by the anointing of the Holy Spirit words that directly impact someone's life. Many Christians would not desire to preach from a pulpit – it is a special calling. Most Christians though will love others with an agape love – the love of God – so they will give, serve, love, encourage and witness Christ to those in their lives. It is your compassion for others, true agape love that can lead others to Christ.

Matthew 22: [37] Jesus said unto him, Thou shalt love the Lord thy God with all thy heart, and with all thy soul, and with all thy mind.

[38] This is the first and great commandment.

[39] And the second is like unto it, Thou shalt love thy neighbour as thyself.

[40] On these two commandments hang all the law and the prophets.

Other Christians many lead groups to Evangelize through dramas or music or concerts or special activities. Large crowds gather at such successful events and hundreds or thousands of people become Christians because of it. Many Churches sponsor such activities.

My own local church sponsors movies, a Christian fun day sort of carnival with clowns, games, music, fireworks etc. free to the people, concerts, dramas. There is evangelism but it is subtle demonstrating to those who don't yet know Christ (pre-Christians) through untraditional ways. There is always a Christian song or scripture or witnessing evangelism. Many people who would not come to a church service, would bring their children to a fun day or a movie. Some will come to church because of such events. They will realize we are regular people and not be intimidated to come.

There are churches that sponsor car washes (free) or other such services so they can share Christ. I've been part of door to door Evangelism with one of my churches. There are also outreaches such as ministry to those in hospital or those in nursing homes, shut ins or those who cannot care for themselves. Evangelism can be administered in many ways, but it must in some way give glory to Jesus Christ. It can be a scripture, a prayer, a song, or some discussions with people by trained leaders.

There must be some sharing of the gospel or it is not evangelism. I know there are some churches that do not preach Christ but serve or host events, they believe they are making a difference; I do not judge them. I am glad for each demonstration of the love of Christ on the earth. The point is there are Christians witnessing to others in a multitude of ways. Use what you've got to share Christ with those in your community or sphere of authority.

There is a literal belief that what we do for others is an expression of our love for Christ. Jesus set the standard for preaching the gospel and how to truly love others in his preaching. In this example he explains that how we respect others, serve others, love others etc. will be a consideration on judgement day. Those who did not give when they could have, will be judged by what they did not do. If you know it is right to give or serve or encourage and you do not, it is sin.

Matthew 25: [31] When the Son of man shall come in his glory, and all the holy angels with him, then shall he sit upon the throne of his glory:

[32] And before him shall be gathered all nations: and he shall separate them one from another, as a shepherd divideth his sheep from the goats:

[33] And he shall set the sheep on his right hand, but the goats on the left.

[34] Then shall the King say unto them on his right hand, Come, ye blessed of my Father, inherit the kingdom prepared for you from the foundation of the world:

³⁵ For I was an hungred, and ye gave me meat: I was thirsty, and ye gave me drink: I was a stranger, and ye took me in:

³⁶ Naked, and ye clothed me: I was sick, and ye visited me: I was in prison, and ye came unto me.

³⁷ Then shall the righteous answer him, saying, Lord, when saw we thee an hungred, and fed thee? or thirsty, and gave thee drink?

³⁸ When saw we thee a stranger, and took thee in? or naked, and clothed thee?

³⁹ Or when saw we thee sick, or in prison, and came unto thee?

⁴⁰ And the King shall answer and say unto them, Verily I say unto you, Inasmuch as ye have done it unto one of the least of these my brethren, ye have done it unto me.

Jesus identifies himself with those who are poor, needy, naked, alone, in prison etc. Many people would consider these people are unimportant or cast a-ways. The truth is Jesus blesses us as we care for others. We don't bless others because we want something, we do it because we love them as we love ourselves.

Those who do not truly love God with all their hearts cannot love others as they love themselves. Only God can give us the agape love of God – the love that only God can give – pure – giving- with no other motive. Those who do not give or serve others when given an opportunity will be judged for it.

⁴¹ Then shall he say also unto them on the left hand, Depart from me, ye cursed, into everlasting fire, prepared for the devil and his angels:

[42] For I was an hungred, and ye gave me no meat: I was thirsty, and ye gave me no drink:

[43] I was a stranger, and ye took me not in: naked, and ye clothed me not: sick, and in prison, and ye visited me not.

[44] Then shall they also answer him, saying, Lord, when saw we thee an hungred, or athirst, or a stranger, or naked, or sick, or in prison, and did not minister unto thee?

[45] Then shall he answer them, saying, Verily I say unto you, Inasmuch as ye did it not to one of the least of these, ye did it not to me.

[46] And these shall go away into everlasting punishment: but the righteous into life eternal.

There are churches, including my own, that sponsor feeding programs for children in schools. As a teacher, I know it is essential that children get a nutritious meal so they can study and learn the curriculum. The truth is many parents do not give breakfast or lunch or their children. It is not the norm but it occurs. Those children would not get proper nutrition (in North America!) if it were not for church sponsored school feeding programs. It may be a donation of money or it may be both the donation of people who willingly go serve breakfast, lunch to children in school. They prepare the food, distribute it and clean up – all unknown to the majority of people. They are evangelizing with the sacrifice of their lives so that children get a chance of succeeding in life. Without proper nutrition, kids can't learn. Education is essential for the hope of a future for all children – especially so of those children living in poverty. In North America an education can get a person a good job with a steady income – they can get out of poverty.

I've known of other churches that sponsor after school programs for children whose parents work. It is right after school until 4:30 or 5pm. The volunteers help the students with their homework, provide snacks and supervise the children at the school – free. There are not many such free things available. Christians can do it knowing that the protection of the children, is essential for their health and well being. Some churches sponsor after school sports programs providing free training in sports as well as supervision in a safe atmosphere. Jesus set the standard for care of children as important.

Matthew 19: [13] Then were there brought unto him little children, that he should put his hands on them, and pray: and the disciples rebuked them.

[14] But Jesus said, Suffer little children, and forbid them not, to come unto me: for of such is the kingdom of heaven.

Jesus pointed to the importance of children. He prayed for them, preached to them, encouraged them. Should there be children in your life, you should be sowing something of Christ into them. You should be encouraging them to develop their talents and their gifts.

Sunday school

Most churches provide children with Christian teaching during the Sunday preaching portion of the adult service. In my church often the children brought friends who came, learned Bible truths, prayed, created things such as paintings or drawings etc. Some churches sponsor pick up ministry bringing children to Sunday school who couldn't go if they didn't get a free ride. There are large churches who bring their ministry into core areas of cities to children who would not get to hear the gospel any other way. Often there are dramas, musicals, puppets, preaching, worshipping, as well as the preaching of the gospel. It is a ray of light in areas where the parents do not yet know Christ. It is a way of touching souls that many people do not recognize as important. Children are no less important than adults.

Proverbs 22: 6Train up a child in the way he should go: and when he is old, he will not depart from it.

Vacation Bible School

Often churches sponsor Vacation Bible School where a week of lessons on a Bible topic are taught, with prayer and praise, Bible preaching and snacks. The children often present a drama or musical performance on the last night where parents are invited. Many parents are glad for a free baby sitter – the church VBS – so they will let their children attend. Many parents will come to see their children in performance that might not come any other way. VBS is an outreach most normal as well as successful in both small or large churches. There is prayer at the end of each Bible class. This is as light that pierces the darkness – it is the light of the gospel of glory. People can accept Christ in their hearts during these occasions. Should you get an opportunity to serve in any of these ministry events, join. Begin serving. Realize it is significant.

Street Evangelism

There are Christians who will share Christ with people on the streets. One of my churches would train the youth to evangelize on Fridays. The youth would get the training – go on the main street where other youth were "hanging out" and share Christ with them. They witnessed to lines of people lined up for downtown bars, theatres etc. Boldness is necessary. It comes stronger with practice. The main message is salvation, but people would pray with those who requested prayer for other things.

As Paul and Silas (Acts 17) witnessed in the everyday atmosphere of Greece – modern day evangelists will share Christ one on one with people on the street. Not everyone wants to hear what you have to say but some are so lonely they are so glad to speak to someone. Others can make life or death decisions based on their encounters of the day. The truth is many teens, youth etc. do not know the truth of God's love for them so they are hurting. They are not feeling content with their lives. Sharing the good news of Jesus offers them a light, a hope for a future. Your encouraging someone, speaking to those no one would speak to is offering life to those who wouldn't get it without Christ.

John 14: 6 Jesus saith unto him, I am the way, the truth, and the life: no man cometh unto the Father, but by me.

Some street preachers – literally preach a gospel message on a street corner. I've witnessed this in large cities such as Toronto, Montreal, New York. The street evangelists draw crowds of people because of their boldness. Often free snacks or sandwiches are given. Many homeless people come to such events. There are alcoholics, drug addicts and others who would never come to a church who would come to a preaching on the street, receive food, receive the message of salvation. The Salvation army was started in such a way by the boldness of William Booth's street preaching. They often play instruments and witness Christ.

Jesus himself preached in open airfields, boats etc. as well as the Temple. Most of the New testament scriptures are him preaching to crowds in the open air. It is easier to do as part of a ministry team, but should you have boldness in Christ with an outgoing personality, you should begin to volunteer for such events.

I've been a part of a church going door to door, singing Christmas Carols, giving a token gift with the address of the church on it, praying for those who wanted prayer. Not everyone received us with gladness. Some rejected it. Some tried to offer us money. We were not collecting money; we were collecting souls. There were some who were in tears, glad to welcome us to pray with them. It was well worth the effort. Some came to church because of it. The ones in tears we prayed for were worth all the ones who shut the door on us. Teens or youth groups can easily organize such events so that there is singing, prayer, giving etc. You would know your life made a difference directly to someone who wanted prayer.

Christian Broadcasting is often an excellent evangelism. People may turn to the channel, receive encouragement, entertainment, as well as Christian preaching. Many people who would not feel comfortable going to a church would watch a Christian tv show. Many thousands of people come to Christ because of it. They will receive Christ in their own living rooms.

Some phone and pray with a free prayer partner. There is a variety of Christian programming, music, theatre, dance, talk shows, preaching, concerts etc. Also, many wholesome Christian movies are broadcast. It is company for a Christian. It can be a life saver for those who don't know what to do. They are making decisions but have no one to talk with. Often the Christian broadcasting speaks to them in a personal way – they are attracted to the light of Christ. There are many Christian Broadcasters. I mention these: TBN, God TV, Glory Star, CBN – all excellent with a variety of preaching, teaching, concerts, dramas, movies etc.

John 8: 12 Then spake Jesus again unto them, saying, I am the light of the world: he that followeth me shall not walk in darkness, but shall have the light of life.

Matthew 5: 14 Ye are the light of the world. A city that is set on an hill cannot be hid.

15 Neither do men light a candle, and put it under a bushel, but on a candlestick; and it giveth light unto all that are in the house.

16 Let your light so shine before men, that they may see your good works, and glorify your Father which is in heaven.

Evangelism is more than a single preacher standing preaching from a pulpit. As many types of situations a human can get in, are as many as the ways of reaching those souls for Christ. I was part of a Christian Baseball team. All manner of life activity can be invaded by the church. I mean it most positively. We can bring the truths of Christ to people through everyday activities, hobbies, talents. The use of the word Evangelism in this part of the book has emphasized the importance of witnessing in North America. Your involvement in church activities as well as other volunteerism can positively impact others for Christ.

Missions

There are countries over seas where billions of people don't know of Jesus. There are millions of people in places we in North America haven't heard of who do not know the truth of Jesus. Christian Missions is an essential aspect of the Church. Those who give themselves as missionaries have one aspect the same. They go to preach Christ. They impact the culture they live in preaching and teaching, living a holy life and being a Christlike example to those people in their spheres of authority.

Some go as preachers; some go as teachers. Some establish training centres. Some feed the hungry, dig freshwater wells so the people get something so essential to human existence – fresh clean water. We in North America take fresh water for granted. In the region I live in there is an abundance of water. In many countries, they do not have the technology or the money to provide clean water for their people. A simple thing such as digging a fresh water well for a community can save lives. It can prevent diseases. It can make it easy for the residents of the village or town. It becomes a source of life for the community. It also demonstrates that we Christians care for their basic life necessities as well as their souls' eternal destiny. Should your church or youth group or Christian organization offer the opportunity for you to go on a mission's trip, I encourage you to go.

Training the people in hygiene, nutrition etc. is often a main element of those in the health care fields along with doctors, nurses, dentists, surgeons etc. Simple things available to us in our culture free (in my country) or cheaply (in other countries) are either too costly or not available in many communities overseas.

There are a multitude of ministries that are missionaries. There are teachers who teach school sharing Christ in other nations. There are skilled trade labourers and unskilled but willing volunteers that will build homes for people, churches, Bible Colleges, schools. All the missionaries either raise their own funds, work to support themselves or are sponsored by others. Most of the missionaries are sponsored by people in North America or Europe. I emphasize in the scripture " that I might by some means save some". Missionaries will use whatever they have to win souls. They pray for finances and resources and receive them.

1 Corinthians 9: [22] To the weak became I as weak, that I might gain the weak: I am made all things to all men, that I might by all means save some.

[23] And this I do for the gospel's sake, that I might be partaker thereof with you.

Lester Summerall, (1913-1996) a man of God who was an excellent preacher, teacher, Apostle, Evangelist lived a humble life as a preacher. He trained many leaders for Christ. I remember him especially for his obedience to God. God spoke to him while he was in Jerusalem. He shared with him that there are Christians in Africa crying out to God for daily food, water, shelter. Many are perishing. God impressed on Summerall that he was to use all means possible to get food, equipment, water, resources to those in Africa. It was a new area for him. He had devoted his life to Evangelism and started churches, build a Bible College – sponsored missions. This was serious. I could hear within his voice the authority of Jesus Christ. Should Christians in North America give the price of one meal a day, we could feed Africa. Christians gave; thousands gave to LeSea Ministries because of it. He was supernaturally blessed. Government donated an old bomber plane that was hulled out and used as a cargo plane. There were large cargo ships donated to the ministry. Huge corporations such as Kellogg's donated extra products such as rice crispies or corn flakes. All of the donations together we a strange combination, yet they supplied for those churches in Africa. The donations were done through the churches. There was accountability without corruption. God used Lester Summerall to connect Christians to give in a specific unique way. His excellent reputation for living as a preacher of the gospel for more than 50 years, was evidence to give him credibility with Christians and others who gave to the ministry. The majority of the cost is in the shipping or transportation of the supplies to Africa. The donation of the cargo transportation was the solution to it. Once a man or woman of God obeys God, the special favour of God comes upon him or her and supernatural provision occurs. He was in his 80's travelling the world, preaching, teaching, training up ministers to do the same.

Some missionaries go for a week, a month, 6 months, a year, 2 years. Some give their lives in missions. I've been privileged to personally know many missionaries. Successful teachers, preachers, doctors, executives, etc. who willingly yield to the promptings of their spirit and go to other nations is something to be respected. Knowing their character, knowing they could have lived a comfortable life in our society with their education and training, yet knowing they sacrificed it so they could bring Christ to other nations is a personal sort of witness. The cost of them giving their lives as missionaries is not cheap but it is most excellent. Often the pay they receive is much less than what their careers could provide in North America. Not all can make the sacrifice or feel the calling to go, so we should give to the gospel so that others may go. Giving to support global missions should be a primary concern for Christians who do not themselves go as missionaries.

1 Corinthians 16: 1 Now concerning the collection for the saints, as I have given order to the churches of Galatia, even so do ye.

2 Upon the first day of the week let every one of you lay by him in store, as God hath prospered him, that there be no gatherings when I come.

2 Corinthians 9 : 6 But this I say, He which soweth sparingly shall reap also sparingly; and he which soweth bountifully shall reap also bountifully.

Missionaries do more than simply preach from a pulpit. Many non- Christians and those who have never known missionaries do not know the importance of Christians in all spheres of society in all nations. There are some evangelists who hold huge crusades of hundreds of thousands or millions of people. Often, they not only preach the gospel so people are saved, healed, delivered, encouraged by the good news of Jesus Christ, the Evangelists have teams of volunteers who pray with people, give Bibles and gospel materials to those who attend. The cost of such Crusades is not cheap, but the results are eternal. Churches are planted, Bible Colleges built, training centers are started. There is a care for all the community and the quality of the lives of the people.

Jesus commanded his disciples to "Go ye into all the world and preach the gospel" (Mark 16: 15) preach the gospel. Jesus Himself brought more than kind words to people. He healed, delivered from oppression, fed the hungry. One of the main signs of Jesus return to earth as he promised is the preaching of the gospel to all the earth. There are thousands of missionaries in many nations. Many risk their lives to go to the countries because Christians are murdered there. There are radical missionaries who believe it is worth it to risk their lives so that a soul can be saved. One salvation can lead to others being saved. Once a person becomes a Christian, his or her life changes – Christ is in him or her and the radiance of Christ cannot be ignored. Others will desire to know Christ.

I've known of missionaries who risk their lives, and are miraculously delivered from death. One of the missionaries to Haiti from our church was in a car on her way to the mission base when a rioting mob surrounded all the vehicles on the road banging on them with sticks and guns. Everyone in the missionary car was praying in the spirit and continued. By some miracle, they passed through the midst of the situation. There are many others who are martyred. The truth is Christianity began with all the disciples being martyred for their faith. It did not stop the Church – it is known as the blood of the martyrs is the seed or the multiplication of the Church.

Matthew 24: [14] And this gospel of the kingdom shall be preached in all the world for a witness unto all nations; and then shall the end come.

Chapter end questions

1. Do you know of any missionaries personally? Explain how their lives impacted you.

2. Would you consider a missionary trip should you go with your church or Christian organization?

3 WHY WE ARE SO PASSIONATE ABOUT THE COMMISSION

Matthew 24: [14] And this gospel of the kingdom shall be preached in all the world for a witness unto all nations; and then shall the end come.

Jesus shall come back as he promised he would. He was on the Mt. of Olives speaking with more than 500 disciples after his resurrection from the dead. He appeared off and on in different places to different people – his disciples for forty days. As he stood preaching to his disciples, he began to ascend up into heaven with 500 or more witnesses. Angels filled the skies. He had promised he would bring his kingdom to the earth for a thousand years. There will be peace. There will be life as heaven on earth.

Acts 1: [10] And while they looked stedfastly toward heaven as he went up, behold, two men stood by them in white apparel;

[11] Which also said, Ye men of Galilee, why stand ye gazing up into heaven? this same Jesus, which is taken up from you into heaven, shall so come in like manner as ye have seen him go into heaven.

A day is coming when Jesus shall return to earth visibly in his resurrected body. People will recognize him by his scars. He will come to earth and establish his throne at Jerusalem in the rebuilt Temple at Jerusalem. There will be peace on earth for a thousand years.

After, there will be the end of all wars as Satan fights against Christ. It will be the shortest war because Satan's destiny was determined at Calvary. Jesus died for humans so we could be free from sin. Jesus blood makes it possible so we can be in communion with God.

Rev 20: 7 And when the thousand years are expired, Satan shall be loosed out of his prison,

8 And shall go out to deceive the nations which are in the four quarters of the earth, Gog, and Magog, to gather them together to battle: the number of whom is as the sand of the sea.

The war will be the armies of God lead by Jesus Christ against those who hate Israel and those who hate God lead by Satan. It will not last long. Jesus will be wearing his authority to execute judgement. Each crown is authority to rule and reign. His blood dipped clothing is the proof of his life as a sacrifice, his blood shed so that those who believe on him can be saved. He will lead the armies of God. The sword in his mouth is the Word of God. Jesus is the Word of God. He is the Word made flesh. (John 1:1) The Word of God has authority over all of earth. Jesus is coming as a mighty champion. He is coming as a warrior King.

Revelation 19: 11 And I saw heaven opened, and behold a white horse; and he that sat upon him was called Faithful and True, and in righteousness he doth judge and make war.

12 His eyes were as a flame of fire, and on his head were many crowns; and he had a name written, that no man knew, but he himself.

13 And he was clothed with a vesture dipped in blood: and his name is called The Word of God.

14 And the armies which were in heaven followed him upon white horses, clothed in fine linen, white and clean.

15 And out of his mouth goeth a sharp sword, that with it he should smite the nations: and he shall rule them with a rod of iron: and he treadeth the winepress of the fierceness and wrath of Almighty God.

16 And he hath on his vesture and on his thigh a name written, KING OF KINGS, AND LORD OF LORDS.

Revelation 20: 9 And they went up on the breadth of the earth, and compassed the camp of the saints about, and the beloved city: and fire came down from God out of heaven, and devoured them.

10 And the devil that deceived them was cast into the lake of fire and brimstone, where the beast and the false prophet are, and shall be tormented day and night for ever and ever.

Finally. The judgement shall be complete. Death, hell, the grave – will be no more. Satan is judged. He is sentenced eternally. Those who hated God, murders, thieves, sinners who would not accept Jesus as their Saviour, will be with Satan. Those who rejected God, will go there.

The New Jerusalem

Our destiny is not heaven. Our destiny is not on the earth as we know it. Our destiny is the New Jerusalem. There will be a new heavens, a new earth. The new Jerusalem shall be on the new earth – literally heaven shall be on the earth. All who received Christ shall go there. It will be a new beginning. It will be without sin or sickness or sorrow. Jesus will live in the midst of us.

Revelation 21:1 And I saw a new heaven and a new earth: for the first heaven and the first earth were passed away; and there was no more sea.

2 And I John saw the holy city, new Jerusalem, coming down from God out of heaven, prepared as a bride adorned for her husband.

3 And I heard a great voice out of heaven saying, Behold, the tabernacle of God is with men, and he will dwell with them, and they shall be his people, and God himself shall be with them, and be their God.

4 And God shall wipe away all tears from their eyes; and there shall be no more death, neither sorrow, nor crying, neither shall there be any more pain: for the former things are passed away.

5 And he that sat upon the throne said, Behold, I make all things new. And he said unto me, Write: for these words are true and faithful.

There shall be nations. There shall be some similarities to the earth we have known. It is a kingdom of light.

Revelation 21: 24 And the nations of them which are saved shall walk in the light of it: and the kings of the earth do bring their glory and honour into it.

25 And the gates of it shall not be shut at all by day: for there shall be no night there.

26 And they shall bring the glory and honour of the nations into it.

27 And there shall in no wise enter into it any thing that defileth, neither whatsoever worketh abomination, or maketh a lie: but they which are written in the Lamb's book of life.

There will only be eternal life, peace, prosperity, joy, life in communion with God. This truth must be shared with the nations. If they do not know the truth of Jesus sacrifice, they cannot choose Jesus. All people living must get the chance to know the truth of Jesus. As Christians, it is our responsibility to share Christ with as many people as possible.

Matthew 28: 18 And Jesus came and spake unto them, saying, All power is given unto me in heaven and in earth.

19 Go ye therefore, and teach all nations, baptizing them in the name of the Father, and of the Son, and of the Holy Ghost:

20 Teaching them to observe all things whatsoever I have commanded you: and, lo, I am with you always, even unto the end of the world. Amen.

Chapter end questions

1. From 1- 10 with 10 being hot how would you rate your passion for the commission?

2. List your activities as they relate to evangelism. Missions. Is your involvement temporary or would you continue doing the activities?

3. What opportunities does your Church or Christian organization give for missionary serving? Did you consider it?

4 PREPARING YOURSELF

Maybe you 've received Christ and feel a strong tug at your heart to serve Him in a special way but you don't know what to do. I know I was in that very position after I received Christ. I was serious, I would give my life. I would have gone anywhere or done anything to honour God. I was a student in school. I remember not knowing what I should do and praying about it. I didn't know if I should continue school or not. I clearly received a word from God. It comforted me. I realized God wanted me to continue my studies as I had planned. From this experience, I learned to pray regarding all serious commitments of my life.

1 Corinthians 7: [20] Let every man abide in the same calling wherein he was called.

I graduated and became a teacher. I did not immediately get a job as a teacher. I got a part time job that paid well but it was part time. It was necessary for me to do many types of manual labour to support myself. I painted, dug ditches, dig roofing, sold vacuums etc.

I studied Bible classes as much as I could. I knew that I would be ministering in the Church. I took years of Bible studies. Later, I took Minister's Candidate School and Minister's training school, ways of entering into ministry. I began teaching Sunday School, Vacation Bible School. I was entrusted with more authority in different aspects of teaching and ministering the Word – supporting myself as a teacher. I was entrusted to preach to the congregation. I was entrusted to give my testimony to groups of women to lead Youth. I did whatever opportunity arose for myself (praying seriously about each one). I served in many different areas of the church teaching preschool to adults during my life. I realized that I didn't know the way to the next things in my life – but I believed God would direct my step and bless me and he has. A phrase rose up in my spirit and I live by it. I recommend it to you.

Do what you can do with all your might, until the next thing is revealed to you.

If you are a student, do it with excellence. Should you be a truck drover, do it with excellence. Whatever your profession is – continue in it with excellence and God will provide opportunities for your success in ministry should you feel the calling. Should you apply yourself wholly to your present situation, you will be promoted. There will be opportunities for you. As each opportunity presents itself, pray over it – God will direct your steps, your paths.

Proverbs 3: [6] In all thy ways acknowledge him, and he shall direct thy paths.

Colossians 3: [23] And whatsoever ye do, do it heartily, as to the Lord, and not unto men;

[24] Knowing that of the Lord ye shall receive the reward of the inheritance: for ye serve the Lord Christ.

Education

Without a high school diploma, life in North America would be tough financially. In other countries, it would mean poverty. In North America we have the freedom of free education until 12th grade. Afterwards, there are grants of money for students, Bursaries, student loans, a Diploma or Degree, awards and scholarships that can help people who could never afford to get higher education. Without a College Diploma or University Degree jobs available are scarce. I myself was able to get advanced education because of government loans and grants. Without the money, I would not have the education or the job I've got now. It took a chunk of my life paying back the money I owed, but it is worth it. There were awards and special jobs for Graduate Students. My education is a result of much prayer on my part, much effort on my part and the freedom in North America to obtain education and honouring of the value of education.

As a teacher, I often see students who are juggling part time jobs so they can get their diploma or degree. I always encourage them. There is personal sacrifice in obtaining higher education but without it, the chances of getting a high paying career are impossible. My advise to you is that you obtain diplomas, degrees, certificates, training etc. The more credentials you obtain, the more opportunities you will get to use being a light for Christ.

In my book Living Life Fully, I direct the book towards students who are interested in a career but don't know what to choose. I highly recommend that book to you. It examines the Spiritual gifts – so Students can know their spiritual giftings and purpose in the Body of Christ, as well as practical advise for youth, 20'somethings and 30'somethings towards getting a job. You might be interested should you be entering retraining for a new career. The book is practical from a Christian Teacher's point of view. The book is inspirational in that it helps you identify your gifts and talents. Knowing your strengths is essential to getting a career and serving Christ. You must know what you want before you can obtain it.

Should you go up to a counter at a McDonald's and the cashier asks what you want and you respond – I don't know. I hope it is good. I pray it is good. If you do that it is ridiculous. You won't get a Big Mac. You won't get a hamburger or anything. Similar is this example. I like archery quite a bit. I'm pretty good at it also. I like shooting at targets not animals. I could hit the target pretty much because of practice. Should I not see the target or aim at something else, I will not hit the target. I must aim at the target to hit the target. Any of you who have shot with a gun or rifle or arrow know what I am talking about. Whether it be a video game shoot or a bow and arrow, you must aim at your target to hit it. Whether it is a teacher or a hairdresser or a truck driver or a scientist, if you do not aim yourself in that direction, you will never achieve it. You must aim yourself in education also. You must aim at a specific career. You must aim in a certain area of ministry.

Aptitudes

The best way to aim yourself is to take an aptitude test at your high school. If you are an adult returning to school, you can get that aptitude at the college or university. It is given through the Student services. It is free. It is a long list that asks you what your interests are. There as a component that shows where your strengths are. It is necessary to know yourself and what your strengths are before you attempt anything. I've known of students who go to school, juggling jobs who put the effort into it, but the area is not one of interest or of strength and they fail. You should not simply gamble with your career. The things you enjoy the most are a determiner of your strengths.

Prayer is essential. Pray that God will give you wisdom. Pray that God will connect you with the right connections. Your spiritual life is important but there is a practical common sense aspect to pursuing your career. The gifts and talents within you, your interests and aptitudes can determine a path that is worth investigating.

As an example, I share with you, I wanted to be a teacher since I was a child; I started teaching my stuffed animals at the age of 2 or 3. Once I learned to read some words, I started teaching kids younger than myself to read books. I've always enjoyed teaching. There were other interests, but my main interest was teaching. The aptitudes showed it was a wise choice. The interest was there. It is the path I chose. Once I became a Christian, I desired to preach and teach the gospel. The aptitude is there. The interest is there. I pursued Minister's Candidate school and Minister's training school.

Get education. Get the most education you can. There are so many careers that people don't even know exist. Search the Internet for a list of careers. You will see that within teaching there are hundreds of different kinds of teachers. Within the realm of teaching/preaching the gospel there are hundreds of kinds of ministers. I've known of students who wanted to be nurses but couldn't academically achieve it – but, they could focus their efforts in some other area of health care. Or they could get specialized tutoring to achieve their nursing career.

Get Education. It's a priority.

Get all the Bible training and classes you can. Large Churches offer many classes you can take to learn more about Christ. Develop yourself in the Word of God. I've been so honoured to receive excellent Christian Education. Each year of my life since I've been a Christian, I was either studying a Bible class, teaching a Bible class or studying for ministry and teaching Bible classes. The ministry study, I did in the evenings. I was preparing for my future in ministry. Because of my sacrifice, I was able to get promoted in my churches teaching Sunday school, Teaching College and Career, preaching from the pulpit, launching a Bible class on the essentials of the Christian faith. I've been entrusted to lead others who were pursuing ministry training.

2 Timothy 2:²And the things that thou hast heard of me among many witnesses, the same commit thou to faithful men, who shall be able to teach others also.

Keep self improvement – as a priority. I read a book several years ago that radically changed myself in my home life habits. It is Intentional Living by John Maxwell. He is a Christian author, speaker, communicator leader. He launches seminars to corporations as well as Christian organizations. In the book he emphasizes living your life for others – adding value by using your gifts, talents, education etc. to serve others and train others. He emphasizes continuous self development or growth through reading, taking classes, getting audios in your strength zone. Keep improving. Keep serving, training up others.

The main thing Maxwell emphasizes- that has impacted my life is professional/personal development in an area of your strength 1 hour a day. He gives the example that within years you could learn a new language that way. You can build your repertoire of stories and antidotes etc. Making a commitment to continue training once you obtain your career is essential.

I apply continual development both in professional development and in areas of my personal strengths. Getting new, creative ideas from various aspects of your life refreshes you and helps you to do both your career and your ministry effectively. I also study in areas of interest and areas new to me so that I am learning of other things, but the majority of my efforts are towards the areas of my strengths.

You and The Commission

If you haven't made the commission your own – receive it as your own. Insert your own name and say it over yourself.

Matthew 28: [19] Go ye therefore, and teach all nations, baptizing them in the name of the Father, and of the Son, and of the Holy Ghost:

[20] Teaching them to observe all things whatsoever I have commanded you: and, lo, I am with you always, even unto the end of the world. Amen.

Say it, "I am to go preach the gospel to all nations." Own the commission. Jesus fulfilled all Messianic prophecies. He is Messiah. His life proved the scriptures. Without Christ we are nothing, but we are not without Christ. Jesus lives within us. His Holy Spirit is in us empowering us.

Matthew 9: [26] But Jesus beheld them, and said unto them, With men this is impossible; but with God all things are possible.

These were the words Jesus quoted as he revealed Himself as Messiah in Luke 4: 18.

Jesus fulfilled all these scriptures and many others. It was His purpose. He identified the reason for the Holy Spirit upon Him was to preach the good news. The Good news is salvation of the soul – eternal life, peace, joy, abundance the blessings of the Abrahamic covenant.

BLESSINGS OF ABRAHAMIC COVENANT

Genesis 2: ²And I will make of thee a great nation, and I will bless thee, and make thy name great; and thou shalt be a blessing:

³And I will bless them that bless thee, and curse him that curseth thee: and in thee shall all families of the earth be blessed.

God promised to bless him in all his ways. God promised to fight against his enemies. God promised him that he would become a strong nation with so many descendants they would be as numerous as the stars in the sky or the grains of sand on a beach. Sarah gave birth at the age of nearly 90 years old. Issac prospered inheriting the blessings of Abraham – Jacob his son became Israel – his name chosen by God. Jacob/Israel was the start of the nation of Israel. His 12 sons become 12 tribes. Israel became a people of millions.

THE BLESSINGS OF THE MOSAIC COVENENANT

The blessings of the Mosaic Covenant are listed throughout the books of the Torah but of special significance a summary can be found in Deuteronomy. We , as Christians , become engrafted into Jesus Christ. We inherit all the blessings by faith in Jesus

Christ. Jesus is living seated on the throne of glory. Jesus is living in the person of the Holy Spirit in all Christians.

God promised to bless Israel through their obedience to His Word. The commandments were given. There are 613 Levitical laws. Each of these things, the Israelites must obey. Their obedience meant that God would make them a nation of reputation. God's blessing would be upon them, and overtake them. That means the blessings would be following them wherever they went – the blessings would not only follow them but overtake them – as if two were running and the one behind ran past the first. Blessings are the result of obedience to God's Word.

Deuteronomy 28:1 And it shall come to pass, if thou shalt hearken diligently unto the voice of the LORD thy God, to observe and to do all his commandments which I command thee this day, that the LORD thy God will set thee on high above all nations of the earth:

2 And all these blessings shall come on thee, and overtake thee, if thou shalt hearken unto the voice of the LORD thy God.

3 Blessed shalt thou be in the city, and blessed shalt thou be in the field.

4 Blessed shall be the fruit of thy body, and the fruit of thy ground, and the fruit of thy cattle, the increase of thy kine, and the flocks of thy sheep.

5 Blessed shall be thy basket and thy store.

In these verses there is a promise that wherever Israel should go, she should be blessed- God promised to bless the children and the animals, their goods, their banks or storage. God promised to bless them either coming or going. That means every place Israelites would go the blessing would be upon them – supernatural favour.

⁶ Blessed shalt thou be when thou comest in, and blessed shalt thou be when thou goest out.

God promised to fight against Israel's enemies scattering them. God commanded the blessing on Israel. As sure as God commanded Israel to love God with all might, power, strength, He commanded the blessing on Israel.

⁷ The LORD shall cause thine enemies that rise up against thee to be smitten before thy face: they shall come out against thee one way, and flee before thee seven ways.

⁸ The LORD shall command the blessing upon thee in thy storehouses, and in all that thou settest thine hand unto; and he shall bless thee in the land which the LORD thy God giveth thee.

God established Israel as a peculiar people – meaning special. They were the people God chose to reveal Himself to as God. The blessing on Israel would be so strong that other nations would fear Israel.

⁹ The LORD shall establish thee an holy people unto himself, as he hath sworn unto thee, if thou shalt keep the commandments of the LORD thy God, and walk in his ways.

¹⁰ And all people of the earth shall see that thou art called by the name of the LORD; and they shall be afraid of thee.

God's covenant is to bless – with abundance of prosperity financially, in their homes, in their careers, their livestock. God's treasures would be given unto Israel. God would send rain upon their land. God would cause Israel to be so prosperous that Israel could lend to others. God would raise them to the highest place – Israel would always rise above the other nations. The covenant promise is dependent upon Israel obeying God's Word.

11 And the Lord shall make thee plenteous in goods, in the fruit of thy body, and in the fruit of thy cattle, and in the fruit of thy ground, in the land which the Lord sware unto thy fathers to give thee.

12 The Lord shall open unto thee his good treasure, the heaven to give the rain unto thy land in his season, and to bless all the work of thine hand: and thou shalt lend unto many nations, and thou shalt not borrow.

13 And the Lord shall make thee the head, and not the tail; and thou shalt be above only, and thou shalt not be beneath; if that thou hearken unto the commandments of the Lord thy God, which I command thee this day, to observe and to do them:

This is the necessary part Israel must keep. It in itself is also a blessing because keeping the Word of God with passion and zeal – living in the Covenant – is a blessing in itself. It is the result of God's mercy that we can obey His Word.

14 And thou shalt not go aside from any of the words which I command thee this day, to the right hand, or to the left, to go after other gods to serve them.

IDENTIFICATION WITH JESUS - CONCERNING THE COMMISSION

This passage of Scripture is an example of the Messianic prophecies Jesus lived. Jesus can heal the spirit soul body of a person. Jesus can deliver a person from sin, addiction. Jesus sets people free.

Isiah 61:1 The Spirit of the Lord GOD is upon me; because the LORD hath anointed me to preach good tidings unto the meek; he hath sent me to bind up the brokenhearted, to proclaim liberty to the captives, and the opening of the prison to them that are bound;

2 To proclaim the acceptable year of the LORD, and the day of vengeance of our God; to comfort all that mourn;

Now is the day of salvation (2 Corinthians 6: 2) Jesus is in the present. God is omnipresent – past, present – future – because God is eternal. God's mercy is continuous present. His salvation is free. His salvation is available to all who would believe in Jesus. Jesus shed blood means we can receive all of the blessings listed in these scriptures. It means the blessings of the Abrahamic Covenant and the Mosaic Covenant are ours by faith in Jesus Christ's blood.

3 To appoint unto them that mourn in Zion, to give unto them beauty for ashes, the oil of joy for mourning, the garment of praise for the spirit of heaviness; that they might be called trees of righteousness, the planting of the LORD, that he might be glorified.

Beauty for ashes – even if it seems that life is ashes – a divorce, the death of a loved one – a tragedy such as these – God can resurrect your life out of the ashes and make it beautiful. It means trusting God with all your life. It means crying, praying, believing God's word and letting God engraft the Word of God into your life. Jesus Christ heals you spirit, soul, body. It will be as though even though it happened, it will seem as nothing important compared to the joy released in your life. You will laugh with joy. Your life will be blessed. It means living the Word of God.

Getting the Word of God in you releases the gift of faith. Faith comes by hearing and hearing the word of God. Romans 10: 17

The oil of joy for mourning – The death of a loved one or a divorce or those types of life changing things are never the end for a Christian. A new beginning can occur. It is total trust in Christ. It is radical Christian living – getting the Word of God in you by listening to Cds, preaching, teaching, worshipping, praying, Speaking God's word, developing your interests and receiving wholeness from Christ. It means growth. You will be renewed, stronger. You will want to try new things, enjoy your life in different ways. You might travel. You might take up a new hobby or take classes.

My friend, upon her divorce, immediately invested in herself and did a second Master's degree. She invested in herself spiritually as well. She grew in Christ. She did not give in to self pity. She realized she must turn to Christ with all her being. She had been already serving Christ – this only caused her to get more radical for Christ. She became a spiritual covering for her children praying for them, with them and sowing spiritually into each of their lives.

Should you be in a position where you can personally relate to the scripture, you should be encouraged knowing there are others, millions of others who have been healed by Jesus Christ. You can also. Develop both spiritual and natural talents and pursue your life. God can bring a new spouse in your life should you desire it. I've known of those who pursue their lives and God brings someone else into their life. There are no replacements. There can never be the same person, but you can have someone even more special. It won't be the same. It might be the end of that career you loved, but God can bring you to a career either as awesome or more than you could have hoped for. Believe in Christ – more than anything – its by faith you can go beyond your situation.

Jeremiah 29: 11 For I know the plans I have for you, says the Lord. They are plans for good and not for evil, to give you a future and a hope.

Garment of praise – heaviness

Do not let sorrow or self pity get in you. Instead focus on the positive aspects of your life. What you focus on becomes more important. Set yourself on Christ. Worship, praise God. Learn to dance. Worship God with all your spirit, soul, body. The joy of Christ will fill you. You are overwhelmed with the goodness of God.

Isaiah 61:4 And they shall build the old wastes, they shall raise up the former desolations, and they shall repair the waste cities, the desolations of many generations.

Your life can be built in a new way, in a creative way, beyond what you have known. God can anoint you to a resurrected life.

This truth – the promises of this Scripture of the Messiah, Jesus lived , you must embrace with all your spirit. You must believe it. You must receive it. If you believe, if you receive, you will be living a miracle. You shall become a living epistle – or a living scripture. The Word can be yours. Should you be sharing Christ with somebody, you must know that you know Christ is life. He is the way, the truth, the life (John 14: 6) Should you receive this type of miracle, you must share it with others so they can be saved, healed, delivered etc.

As you literally believe God's Word – and have experienced it – your life becomes a testimony to share with others so you can bring life to others. We Christians must identify with the scripture. It is our mandate. Jesus Christ is saviour, healer, baptizer, deliverer.

New Covenant blessings mean forgiveness of sin, life eternal, inheriting the blessings of The Abrahamic Covenant as well as the blessings of the Mosaic Covenant. It is Jesus the Messiah that gives us right standing with God. This is the gospel of Jesus Christ. This is the gospel we must share with others. First you must believe it; You must preach it. You must live it.

Chapter end questions

1. Briefly explain the Abrahamic Covenant.

2. Briefly explain the Mosaic Covenant.

3. Are you living in the blessing as discussed in this chapter? Explain.

5 SPHERES OF AUTHORITY

Career

Once you've got your career, you've got a new sphere of authority. Use all your efforts to preach, teach, live the gospel, serve, doing your job as though you are doing it for Christ.

Colossians 3: [23] And whatsoever ye do, do it heartily, as to the Lord, and not unto men;

Submit your life to Christ – expecting God to use you in your sphere of authority

Spheres of authority – Do what you can do serving as many individuals as possible. The more people you encourage, give gifts to, pray with, mentor, serve etc. the more are impacted for Christ. You've got the chance each day to encourage, build up, enlighten inspire others in your life. Start with a smile, a joke, but point to Jesus in some way. It could be a scripture or something God has recently done for you.

There are 7 spheres of Authority identified by Bright and Cunnigham (1999 Youth with a Mission) that are mission fields within society that Christians are part of. Authority in these spheres comes through education, training, experience.

The Spheres of Society

Education - Those in education are teachers of course but also secretaries and support staff as well as administration. A career in education directly impacts the lives of thousands. People in this field enjoy being with others, have strong communication skills.

Teachers can take complex information and dive it into teachable units. Words from teachers or workers in education can deeply impact a student's life positively or negatively. Teachers must obtain degrees in Teaching as well as other subjects. Support staff may have degrees but the minimum requirement is a College diploma. Aptitude in communication is essential. Desire for life long learning makes an excellent teacher.

Economy/business – These careers include all manner of business from management to sales and cashiers. Once more their attitude is essential as they directly work with diverse types of people. Oral and written Communication skills are essential. Business mathematics is necessary as well as persuasive communications. Those in Business at management levels require degrees. Sales representatives may be students. Successful entrepreneurs are those who can comprehend the economy, know the needs of a community and launch a successful business to serve it. Aptitude in business mathematics, communication skills and persuasive skills is necessary.

Media – Those in media are writers, script writers, television hosts, anchor men or women, sportscasters, weather reporters etc. There are others that are necessary to the sphere such as camera operators, recording studio crew, advertising sales' people etc. A diploma or degree is necessary for success in the field. Aptitude at interpreting and communication skills is necessary.

Entertainment – Singers, songwriters, musicians, actors, dancers, film directors, producers etc. are in this field. The requirement is some special talent of exceptional quality. Appearance is important. Many people sculpt a particular image of themselves to show themselves unique whether it be by dress, hair or other outward adornments. It is necessary that these people connect with others to become successful. Study of instruments or the dramatic arts is necessary. Often large successful schools connect students with agents and opportunities. There are a multitude of positions in bars and local places for entertainers. To be recognized nationally, is more rare. Talent without connections and opportunities, is not enough to become successful. Aptitude in talent of the arts is necessary.

Health care – Health care professions are doctors, specialists, nurses, technicians and so many other types of service workers essential to the field. A college diploma is necessary for all technicians. Multiple degrees and longer study is necessary for those in more authoritative fields. The people in this sphere must enjoy serving others concerning well being. There are so many tangent fields such as technicians who implement, interpret and report data concerning patients. Receptionists, emergency response teams etc. Aptitudes necessary are as follows: in science, biology, business mathematics, strong communication skills.

Science/technology – There are many levels of it. Some are teachers or professors. Some are researchers. Some interpret data. There are many specialized interests. Some many spend their life seeking a cure for cancer or some such thing. There are specialists that protect wildlife, study human and animal behaviour. There are those who study the planets and those who develop the means to travel to other planets. It is a vast field. Advanced degrees are necessary for higher levels of science. Aptitude with mathematics, science, biology, chemistry, physics etc. are necessary. Communication skills are essential.

Government – There are diverse types of government. Leaders of nations, provinces or states, cities, schools, regions, companies, corporations etc. Strong leadership skills are necessary. Strong communication skills, self esteem, ability to interpret and create plans based on complex data is necessary for success. The impact of a strong positive leader can turn the direction of a nation. The same is true for a poor leader. Specific education is necessary for the positions. Degrees are necessary. There are many tangent jobs such as secretaries, press people, data collectors, communications dept. personnel etc. Those positions may accept a College Diploma or a degree. Aptitude in communications, studying the economy, mathematics, budgeting, technology, comprehending different types of people groups etc. is necessary for success.

There are levels of authority. You can impact those in your sphere of authority by witnessing Christ. By your spiritual gifts and talents as well as training, education spiritual fruit – impact someone's life. Your smile, attitude, service, excellence can make a difference.

Levels- Your entry position in any of the spheres gives you a realm of authority or connections you can impact by your decisions, excellence and authority. The number of people you connect with, the depth of decision making, the widespread reverberations of your decisions determine your authority in the natural realm. In the spiritual realm, your authority is in Christ.

Authority in Christ – Although you may be a clerk or secretary, your prayers can impact all of the company and those it serves. It is your direct knowledge of things particular to your career, that gives you the prompting to pray specifically. The blood of Jesus

Christ gives you authority to pray for peace, prosperity, blessing, favour, etc. over your coworkers, your bosses, your clients. Should it be possible, get in a prayer group at your business. I've known of secretaries who get together during lunch to pray, share scripture etc. Whatever your sphere of influence, pray for other Christians to be released. Be excellent in your position. That is serve with excellence as unto Christ. Do your tasks but go beyond the normal, do extra. Be known as the most efficient and you will be promoted. It is essential that Christians are excellent in their reputation. You represent the King of Kings. Live your life accordingly.

Ephesians 6: [18] Praying always with all prayer and supplication in the Spirit, and watching thereunto with all perseverance and supplication for all saints;

James 5:16 b The earnest prayer of a righteous man has great power and wonderful results.

Matthew 18: [19] "I also tell you this—if two of you agree down here on earth concerning anything you ask for, my Father in heaven will do it for you. [20] For where two or three gather together because they are mine, I will be right there among them."

Ephesians 4: [11] And he gave some, apostles; and some, prophets; and some, evangelists; and some, pastors and teachers;

[12] For the perfecting of the saints, for the work of the ministry, for the edifying of the body of Christ:

[13] Till we all come in the unity of the faith, and of the knowledge of the Son of God, unto a perfect man, unto the measure of the stature of the fulness of Christ:

Apostles, prophets, evangelists, pastors teachers

Apostles plant churches, ministries, train leaders. They train up other leaders. There are usually signs and wonders in their ministries. There is a special charismatic anointing on them to attract people. They delight in new things, new churches, missionary organizations, Bible Colleges and training centers. As Paul the Apostle planted churches, so Apostles also plant churches train pastors. They have excellent Bible training, education, knowledge and teach the Doctrines of Christ, the foundations etc. They mentor new leaders as Paul trained Timothy and launched him into ministry.

Prophets hear what God is speaking to the Church and share those words with the congregations. They are intercessors. They never contradict God's Word. They honour God and often consecrate their lives in unusual ways. They speak messages from God to the congregation, to leaders, to individuals. They never contradict God's written Word. Almost always there are words of exhortation, edification, comfort – encouragement. Sometimes they rebuke people who are in sin or unbelief. It is essential to obey the words of true prophets. As Moses spoke God's Word to Israel, when Israel obeyed, she prospered. When Israel disobeyed, she suffered. If your spirit does not agree with the prophetic word, don't receive it. Write it on a paper, save it if it aligns with Scripture. If it was a true prophecy, it will come to pass. If does not align with scripture, it is not a true prophecy.

Pastors devote themselves to studying Scripture preaching to a congregation, prayer, service etc. They often make lifelong commitments to a congregation. Pastors are shepherds of God's people. They do routine but necessary things such as teaching, water Baptism, baby dedication, weddings, funerals etc. They can prepare a sermon and present it so that the congregation of different levels of maturity receive something. Often God directs them in their studies so the Church is built, established, encouraged, strengthened. They know the sheep; the sheep know them (John 10:10). There is a deep sacred bond between pastor and the congregation.

Evangelists preach with passion and zeal. They preach salvation, healing, deliverance and prosperity of the Covenant of God. Some are specific over regions or nations. Some are International. Philip was an Evangelist; he obeyed God – he preached to an Etheopian Eunich was saved, baptized and brought the truths of Christ to his nation. Evangelists bring essential truths to their nation. Salvation, healing, deliverance and prosperity are their main topics. Many are known for their healing ministries. T.L. Osborn, Reinhard Bonnke, Benny Hinn are some that operate in the supernatural gifts of the Spirit.

Teachers study the scriptures, often studying Greek or Hebrew. They teach the Word of God in Churches, seminars etc. They are devoted to the scriptures. They have the ability to teach complex truths in simple ways so ordinary people can understand. They are excellent communicators effectively sharing God's Word. They study the Bible; some are proficient in Greek or Hebrew. Some teachers teach adults; some teach Sunday school or vacation Bible school.

Servants, enjoy helping others with practical things such as cleaning, cooking, mowing lawns etc. They desire to help others in practical ways to relieve others. They may babysit so the parents can attend church or a seminar.

1 Corinthains 12: [7] But the manifestation of the Spirit is given to every man to profit withal.

[8] For to one is given by the Spirit the word of wisdom; to another the word of knowledge by the same Spirit;

[9] To another faith by the same Spirit; to another the gifts of healing by the same Spirit;

[10] To another the working of miracles; to another prophecy; to another discerning of spirits; to another divers kinds of tongues; to another the interpretation of tongues:

[11] But all these worketh that one and the selfsame Spirit, dividing to every man severally as he will.

[12] For as the body is one, and hath many members, and all the members of that one body, being many, are one body: so also is Christ.

Romans 12: [6] Having then gifts differing according to the grace that is given to us, whether prophecy, let us prophesy according to the proportion of faith;

[7] Or ministry, let us wait on our ministering: or he that teacheth, on teaching;

[8] Or he that exhorteth, on exhortation: he that giveth, let him do it with simplicity; he that ruleth, with diligence; he that sheweth mercy, with cheerfulness.

Encouragers take pleasure in speaking encouraging words to make a difference to individuals. A word of scripture or a scriptural truth is often on their lips. They can discern when someone needs encouragement. They can often think of steps to get someone out of a rut. They suggest improvements.

Mercy ministry: They show mercy in practical ways such as listening, reading scriptures, praying etc. They are excellent listeners and enjoy speaking with people. They are attracted to those who are hurting. They bring comfort with words, deeds.

Givers give financially to the gospel. They can get money easily and sow it into their churches and other ministries. They have a passion for the great commission and their giving often encourages others giving. They may do match funding campaigns. They may be generous with all the people in their sphere. They especially have a desire to launch missionaries, build churches, give so God's Word can be established in the earth.

Intercessors are especially interested in praying for the concerns of others. Intercessors enjoy the presence of God. Intercessors sacrifice of themselves to pray for the needs of others. It is their joy to pray for others blessing.

Gifts of the Spirit – faith – Those with the gift of faith can believe for miracles. The gift of faith can impart supernatural faith to believe for extraordinary things.

Working of miracles – It is the obedience to God in receiving of miracles. There is a receiving of instruction, and an obedience to instruction.

Gifts of healing – Those with the gifts of the healing can pray for others or impart a healing touch that brings healing to people.

Gift of tongues – It is the gift of speaking in other languages whether natural earthly languages they have not learned or heavenly languages.

Gift of Interpretation of tongues – It is the gift of interpreting the tongues spoken whether the speaker himself or herself or of others. God gives the interpretation to the person.

Gift of Prophecy – It is the gift of speaking God's words of encouragement, exhortation or comfort to congregations or individuals.

Covet the gifts of the Spirit – means to desire them passionately. 1 Corinthians 12: [31] But covet earnestly the best gifts: and yet shew I unto you a more excellent way.

Covet means to earnestly desire – to want, to receive. We are not to covet things or people – but we are encouraged to covet spiritual gifts.

Stir up the gifts of the Spirit 2 Tim 1: [6] Wherefore I put thee in remembrance that thou stir up the gift of God, which is in thee by the putting on of my hands.

STIRRING THE GIFTS

It is necessary that you stir up your spiritual gifts. You do it willfully. You pray over yourself and say words such as follows: "I stir the gift of faith." As you pray over yourself stirring up the gifts, you activate the gifts. They are released fresh. It's best to pray with understanding but also pray in tongues. Do it each day, you release potential for God to use you. Offer yourself a living sacrifice. Expect God to use you. Should the opportunity arise, use it to magnify Christ.

Rom 12:1 I beseech you therefore, brethren, by the mercies of God, that ye present your bodies a living sacrifice, holy, acceptable unto God, which is your reasonable service.

2 And be not conformed to this world: but be ye transformed by the renewing of your mind, that ye may prove what is that good, and acceptable, and perfect, will of God.

2 Timothy 1: 6 This being so, I want to remind you to stir into flame the strength and boldness[a] that is in you, that entered into you when I laid my hands upon your head and blessed you. 7 For the Holy Spirit, God's gift, does not want you to be afraid of people, but to be wise and strong, and to love them and enjoy being with them.

WILLINGNESS

Expect God to use you – present yourself for Christ's use. Expect that God will use you. Should an opportunity arise use it to share Christ. Pray with people. Encourage people. Give. Serve. Live a radical Christian life – adding value to others lives. In can be very practical. For instance, you may pray with someone in a place of business. You will be talking with someone, he or she will say something, you can say " I can pray for you." Afterwards, You pray with the person, briefly – but directly about the thing he or she has mentioned. It is simple but can radically impact that person's life.

Be radical for Christ – but normal in that you are friendly kind, generous, gentle, etc.

HEART ATTITUDE

The character of a person is a determiner of our relationships. Godly character is described in scripture. The fruit of the Spirit is the evidence of the Holy Spirit living within you. The fruit of the Spirit are developed through prayer, Bible reading, Church sermons, teaching, worship, responding to altar calls etc.

Love – the Agape (Greek) love of God is the unconditional, supernatural, overflow of love which God loves you with. It cannot be measured. It is overwhelming. You are a Christian, you comprehend what I am trying to describe. It is that same love in us loving others with the love of God that causes people to come to Christ- through us. It is giving, serving, loving as though you love your own self. There is no human equivalent to this type of love.

Galatians 5: [22] But the fruit of the Spirit is love, joy, peace, longsuffering, gentleness, goodness, faith,

[23] Meekness, temperance: against such there is no law.

Ephesians 3: [18-19] and may you be able to feel and understand, as all God's children should, how long, how wide, how deep, and how high his love really is; and to experience this love for yourselves, though it is so great that you will never see the end of it or fully know or understand it. And so at last you will be filled up with God himself.

Joy – The joy of Christ gives you a desire for life. You treasure your life and want to share the joy with others by encouraging others with words, cards, gifts etc. The joy I am speaking of is not conditional. It is based on the Spirit of God living within you. It bubbles up from your spirit, through your soul and effects your life. The joy of Christ is your strength. It is Christ living in you, through you. It makes you an optimist. It causes you to connect with people. You laugh, smile, are funny. Your character is pleasant. It attracts people.

Colossians 1: 26-27 He has kept this secret for centuries and generations past, but now at last it has pleased him to tell it to those who love him and live for him, and the riches and glory of his plan are for you Gentiles, too. And this is the secret: *Christ in your hearts is your only hope of glory.*

Peace – Jesus Christ is the prince of Peace. Jesus' presence is peace. He dwells within you so His presence is in you. Your character should be peaceful. You should not be tossed about by the things of the earth as severe as they may be. You are anchored in Christ. Christ's Peace is evident in Christians.

Mark 4: 39 Then he rebuked the wind and said to the sea, "Quiet down!" And the wind fell, and there was a great calm!

Temperance - endurance – It is the ability to continue in tough situations letting Christ strengthen you. It can be compared to a runner of a Marathon race. This type of runner must go a long distance so he or she must pace the distance. There are spurts of running fast, but there is also maintaining a speed as you are running the majority of the way.

2 Timothy 2: 3 Take your share of suffering as a good soldier of Jesus Christ, just as I do; 4 and as Christ's soldier, do not let yourself become tied up in worldly affairs, for then you cannot

satisfy the one who has enlisted you in his army. ⁵ Follow the Lord's rules for doing his work, just as an athlete either follows the rules or is disqualified and wins no prize. ⁶ Work hard like a farmer who gets paid well if he raises a large crop. ⁷ Think over these three illustrations, and may the Lord help you to understand how they apply to you.

Gentleness – Jesus could speak with children in such as way that they could understand deep spiritual truths. Jesus gathered children. They were comfortable with him. Children are not drawn to people who are angry or of ill temper. Children desire to be with joyful, caring, calm, gentle people. It means you are soft, tender, kind. You could feel comfortable holding a child. This characteristic is often in those with the gift of mercy. These people feel for and care for others encouraging, sharing, bringing cheer.

Ephesians 4: ³² Instead, be kind to each other, tenderhearted, forgiving one another, just as God has forgiven you because you belong to Christ.

Goodness – Goodness is of good nature. It means you are not self-absorbed. It means you are considerate, helpful, compassionate. This is the type of character of Christ that demonstrated in his everyday life teaching, preaching, doing miracles, attending weddings, parties, celebrations, serving, gathering people, feeding people. It was his sincere care for the people of Israel that caused multitudes to come to him.

Matthew 9: ³⁶ But when he saw the multitudes, he was moved with compassion on them, because they fainted, and were scattered abroad, as sheep having no shepherd.

Faith – Each person is given a measure of faith. The best illustration of it is as a grain of mustard seed. It is a small seed brownish yellow in colour. Yet if planted it grows into a tree. Each person has within a seed of faith. The application of your faith in God's Word determines your life.

Matthew 17: 20 And Jesus said unto them, Because of your unbelief: for verily I say unto you, If ye have faith as a grain of mustard seed, ye shall say unto this mountain, Remove hence to yonder place; and it shall remove; and nothing shall be impossible unto you.

Meekness – It is humility. It is honouring God as the source of all gifts and talents. It is honouring God for your success. It is honouring God for finances. It is recognizing the source of your strength – giving glory to God. As a result, you will be blessed beyond what you know.

Spiritual Fruit

Spiritual Fruit is developed over your life. The more you are in the presence of God, the more the more you yield yourself to the Scriptures, the more Christlike you become. You can pray over specific areas for fruit to develop. I've experienced, the more I desire God's presence, the more I desire the Word of God, my character has changed. It is The Holy Spirit living in me, through me, transforming my spirit, my soul, making me a wise steward of my body.

Galatians 5: 22 But the fruit of the Spirit is love, joy, peace, longsuffering, gentleness, goodness, faith,

23 Meekness, temperance: against such there is no law.

2 Corinthians 3: [18] But we all, with open face beholding as in a glass the glory of the Lord, are changed into the same image from glory to glory, even as by the Spirit of the Lord.

Chapter End questions

1. What are your main spiritual gifts?

2. Describe how you are using them.

3. Imagine a way you can use your spiritual gifts more. Write plan to achieve it.

6 CONNECTIONS

The most important aspect of life I would share with someone who desires to become more Christlike is to focus on others. Start giving. Start serving. Start each day with a fresh inner desire to sow something into someone else's life each day. It may be a kind act or service. It may be a gift. It could be writing a cheery card or making a phone call. Your focus on adding value to others by your desire, intention, commission – is the most like God you can become. Pray for opportunities to be a blessing to someone. Should you speak with someone – sow kindness. On purpose leave an impression of the love of God with each person you encounter.

Often it is not the length of your speech but the sincerity of your words that impacts someone. Listening to others is important, not only the words themselves but the expression, tone and emotion. Read body language. All of these things, must come instantly to you – so you can pray for God to reveal these things to make you an effective witness.

Matthew 22: [37] Jesus said unto him, Thou shalt love the Lord thy God with all thy heart, and with all thy soul, and with all thy mind.

[38] This is the first and great commandment.

[39] And the second is like unto it, Thou shalt love thy neighbour as thyself.

REPUTATION –

Your reputation is how you reveal yourself to others. It occurs in your church. You are known for your responsibilities, volunteering, being friendly, etc. It occurs in your workplace or school. It occurs in your everyday dealings with people: words, character, diligence, work ethic, attitude etc. It occurs in your community. The way you value the people that serve you matters. Your expressions, being polite, kind, gentle, funny etc. impact the people around you. In your home your treatment of your family and friends reveals the real you. The aim is that in all these different areas, you remain the same. You maintain a consistent character. Gloria Copeland started a saying that has become one of my core values – it is " In consistency lies the power."

Consistently do good. Consistently live your life as though you are living for Christ in all aspects of your life. The aim is excellence. Should you be consistent in your relationship with God, your relationship with others, you will be known and respected as a Christian.

Colossians 3: [22] Servants, obey in all things your masters according to the flesh; not with eyeservice, as menpleasers; but in singleness of heart, fearing God;

[23] And whatsoever ye do, do it heartily, as to the Lord, and not unto men;

RELATIONSHIPS

List essential qualities of a friend. Describe an excellent friend in terms of these criteria

1) availability, 2) compatibility, 3) listening, 4) giving, 5) serving, 6)sharpening of each other or adding value to one another.

Write a list of your responses. List your closest friends. Now evaluate your friends in terms of those criteria. You should be surrounding yourself with people who value you, as well as add value to you. Numerically rate them (1-5 highest). Now evaluate yourself as a friend towards each of those people.

Proverbs 27: [17]Iron sharpeneth iron; so a man sharpeneth the countenance of his friend.

You can apply the same criteria to each of your relationships. There are a multitude of books on building relationships. My purpose in this chapter is self examination of your giving, serving, treating of others.

1. Listen more than you speak.
2. Respect each person as your own self.
3. Plan meaningful get togethers.

DIVINE CONNECTIONS

Effective relationship building is one of the joys of life. Social Networking doesn't come easy to all people. There are books on social networking – building a list of career relationships. There is social media that can connect you with others. It is wise to give your business card to every person that might be a business connection. Use social media for work, always be professional.

The most awesome social networker, relationship builder I know of is Christ. You should use all available earthly means of communication, pray for opportunities, and make wise decisions. You will not only obtain your position or objective, but you will be in a position to help others. You should use your authority whether in career or church or community etc. to add values to others. It means letting others know about positions or opportunities. It means you offer a hand up to others as well as receive. Keep in a cycle of giving – receiving – giving.

With your Christian connections, pray, leave a word of scripture or gift.

With your other associates, you may speak a word of scripture but use it in everyday language, so it is natural. Speak an interesting antidote Give your business card, a lead on something or some aspect of uniqueness between you such as a joke, or an interesting aspect that could apply to that person's life.

Pray for Divine connections

God can bring the right people into your life for your mutual benefit.

Acts 11: 25- 18-26

Paul had been radically saved and witnessed at Jerusalem. Because he had been a persecutor of Christians, the people hesitated to receive him as a Christian. Paul met the disciples and they were assured he had become a Christian. The Pharisees threatened to kill him; he escaped with his life and went to his hometown of Tarsus. None of the Apostles sought for him or expressed concern regarding him but Barnabas – his name meaning son of consolation – his character proving that it was true sought for Paul. Barnabas realized Paul was a necessary part of preaching and teaching the good news of the gospel. He encouraged him and got him involved in missions right away. The two of them became an awesome team of preachers.

Acts 11: [25] Then Barnabas went to Tarsus to look for Saul, [26] and when he found him, he brought him to Antioch. So for a whole year Barnabas and Saul met with the church and taught great numbers of people. The disciples were called Christians first at Antioch.

It was not a coincidence that Barnabas sought Paul. It was a Divine connection. The two of them preached through out Greece. They spent 2 years preaching and teaching at Antioch and established a strong Christian mission's base there. Apostles, prophets, Evangelists, Pastors and Teachers were involved in the church. Their adventures are described through out a good portion of the Book of Acts. The encouragement of Paul to begin teaching and preaching Christ directly impacted the nations. God used Barnabas to launch Paul into ministry. Although it was Barnabas who sought Paul, Paul was the mainline preacher, witness of Jesus.

1 Kings 17: [7] Some time later the brook dried up because there had been no rain in the land. [8] Then the word of the LORD came to him: [9] "Go at once to Zarephath in the region of Sidon and stay there. I have directed a widow there to supply you with food." [10] So he went to Zarephath. When he came to the town gate, a widow was there gathering sticks. He called to her and asked, "Would you bring me a little water in a jar so I may have a drink?" [11] As she was going to get it, he called, "And bring me, please, a piece of bread."

[12] "As surely as the LORD your God lives," she replied, "I don't have any bread—only a handful of flour in a jar and a little olive

oil in a jug. I am gathering a few sticks to take home and make a meal for myself and my son, that we may eat it—and die."

[13] Elijah said to her, "Don't be afraid. Go home and do as you have said. But first make a small loaf of bread for me from what you have and bring it to me, and then make something for yourself and your son. [14] For this is what the LORD, the God of Israel, says: 'The jar of flour will not be used up and the jug of oil will not run dry until the day the LORD sends rain on the land.'"

[15] She went away and did as Elijah had told her. So there was food every day for Elijah and for the woman and her family. [16] For the jar of flour was not used up and the jug of oil did not run dry, in keeping with the word of the LORD spoken by Elijah.

Elijah the prophet prophesied a drought in his nation and lived in it. God was sustaining him through a brook and also ravens that brought meat, but the brook dried up. This meant the prophet would go without food or water. God spoke to him encouraging him with provision saying he had commanded a widow woman to sustain him. Elijah obeyed God and went to Zarephath. There he saw the widow woman gathering sticks. He spoke to her requesting water. It was true he was thirsty. It was a normal request. The woman being hospitable was getting him a drink of water but then the prophet requested some food also. She spoke that she didn't have enough to last her and her son. Her words were not positive She thought they were going to die in the famine. Elijah commanded her to bring him a small cake first and he promised her if she did, her food and water would run out. It occurred. The meal lasted them. The water sustained them. It was not a coincidence. It was in this instance a miracle of multiplication of her meal until the drought ended. It was provision for her and her son but also the Prophet. It was a Divine connection.

Jesus on the Emmaus road – Luke 24- [13] Now that same day two of them were going to a village called Emmaus, about seven miles[a] from Jerusalem. [14] They were talking with each other about everything that had happened. [15] As they talked and discussed these things with each other, Jesus himself came up and walked along with them; [16] but they were kept from recognizing him.

[17] He asked them, "What are you discussing together as you walk along?"

They stood still, their faces downcast. [18] One of them, named Cleopas, asked him, "Are you the only one visiting Jerusalem who does not know the things that have happened there in these days?"

[19] "What things?" he asked.

"About Jesus of Nazareth," they replied. "He was a prophet, powerful in word and deed before God and all the people. [20] The chief priests and our rulers handed him over to be sentenced to death, and they crucified him; [21] but we had hoped that he was the one who was going to redeem Israel. And what is more, it is the third day since all this took place. [22] In addition, some of our women amazed us. They went to the tomb early this morning [23] but didn't find his body. They came and told us that they had seen a vision of angels, who said he was alive. [24] Then some of our companions went to the tomb and found it just as the women had said, but they did not see Jesus."

[25] He said to them, "How foolish you are, and how slow to believe all that the prophets have spoken! [26] Did not the Messiah have to suffer these things and then enter his glory?" [27] And beginning with Moses and all the Prophets, he explained to them what was said in all the Scriptures concerning himself.

[28] As they approached the village to which they were going, Jesus continued on as if he were going farther. [29] But they urged him strongly, "Stay with us, for it is nearly evening; the day is almost over." So he went in to stay with them.

[30] When he was at the table with them, he took bread, gave thanks, broke it and began to give it to them. [31] Then their eyes were opened and they recognized him, and he disappeared from their sight. [32] They asked each other, "Were not our hearts burning within us while he talked with us on the road and opened the Scriptures to us?"

[33] They got up and returned at once to Jerusalem. There they found the Eleven and those with them, assembled together [34] and saying, "It is true! The Lord has risen and has appeared to Simon." [35] Then the two told what had happened on the way, and how Jesus was recognized by them when he broke the bread.

The last divine connection I speak of is of Jesus Himself after his resurrection. The disciples were grieved after the death of Jesus. Some did not know he had arisen. They didn't understand. Jesus appeared to them in the road they were travelling on as a stranger but companion. As they asked him why they were not positive, they mentioned Jesus and his death. Jesus began preaching to them all the Messianic scriptures that he had fulfilled. His revealing of how Messiah must die as Saviour for His people encouraged them. He was preaching and teaching them – yet they did not know it was he. Finally, as at they took supper together, they recognizing him. Immediately he disappeared. They knew it was Jesus. It changed their journey. It changed their attitude. It changed their beliefs. They returned to Jerusalem and shared with the disciples that Jesus had appeared to them. They were encouraged. It was not a coincidence. As they journeyed, they were making a destiny decision, not going the right way both in direction nor in faith. Jesus appeared in an unusual way bringing life to them.

Divine Connections

God can cause the right person to enter your life at the exact moment that is necessary. The Bible is filled with such instances. Supernatural encounters with Angels, messengers, prophets and others, fill the pages of the Scriptures. It is a study worth pursuing in itself. Consider your own life. Were there instances in your own life where you received news at a moment it was vitally necessary? Did someone come to your rescue? Were there people God placed in your life throughout your life that radically changed your life? Create a list of unexplainable life changing encounters. List as many as you can. Briefly describe them. Share some of them with people who are close to you. These are Divine connections; give glory to God as you share them.

Getting mentored

Elijah and Elisha

The prophet Elijah had been instructed by God to anoint Elisha as a Prophet. Elijah obeyed. His action of casting his mantle or prophetic coat – on him was choosing him. Elisha obeyed. He spent the remainder of his existence as a prophet. First, he was a prophet in training by serving Elijah. He was known as the one who served Elijah. (2 Kings 3: 11) God's method in training leaders is that the new leaders learn from the elders. They serve, live with the person, are trained day by day. They become excellent. It is mentoring. It is investment in others lives. The truths a believer has learned are passed unto others so that the Word of God is preserved.

1 Kings 19: [9] So Elijah went from there and found Elisha son of Shaphat. He was plowing with twelve yoke of oxen, and he himself was driving the twelfth pair. Elijah went up to him and threw his cloak around him. [20] Elisha then left his oxen and ran after Elijah. "Let me kiss my father and mother goodbye," he said, "and then I will come with you."

"Go back," Elijah replied. "What have I done to you?"

[21] So Elisha left him and went back. He took his yoke of oxen and slaughtered them. He burned the plowing equipment to cook the meat and gave it to the people, and they ate. Then he set out to follow Elijah and became his servant.

Paul and Timothy – Paul had witnessed to Timothy and lead him to Christ. Paul, anointed him, prayed over him and prophesied over him and anointed him to pastor a church. The Book of 1 & 2 Timothy are written to encourage him. It is Paul's instructions to

Timothy that we use to train up leaders in our Church today. Timothy and Thessalonians give specific requirements of Christian leaders. Paul's mentorship of Timothy did not stop once Timothy became pastor; Paul continued to speak into his life words of encouragement, exhortation, instruction as the Apostle of the church. His tone with Timothy is very personal and tender.

1 Timothy 1: [2] To Timothy my true son in the faith:

Grace, mercy and peace from God the Father and Christ Jesus our Lord.

1 Timothy 1: [18] Timothy, my son, I am giving you this command in keeping with the prophecies once made about you, so that by recalling them you may fight the battle well, [19] holding on to faith and a good conscience,

Matthew 10: 1 He called His twelve disciples to Him and gave them authority over unclean spirits, to cast them out, and to heal all kinds of sickness and all kinds of disease.

[2] Now the names of the twelve apostles are these: first, Simon, who is called Peter, and Andrew, his brother; James, the son of Zebedee, and John, his brother; [3] Philip and Bartholomew; Thomas, and Matthew, the tax collector; James, the son of Alphaeus; and Lebbaeus, whose surname was Thaddaeus; [4] Simon the Zealot; and Judas Iscariot, who also betrayed Him.

Jesus chose the 12 disciples. They lived with Jesus. They served together. They learned the Scriptures in a unique way because Jesus, the Living Word, was living with them. They prayed with him. They ministered with him and were anointed by Jesus to minister. Jesus commanded them to preach the kingdom of God. They were anointed and sent while Jesus lived among them.

Matthew 10: [5] These twelve Jesus sent out, and commanded them, saying, "Do not go into the way of the Gentiles, and do not enter any city of the Samaritans. [6] But go rather to the lost sheep of the house of Israel. [7] As you go, preach, saying, 'The kingdom of heaven is at hand.' [8] Heal the sick, cleanse the lepers, raise the dead, and cast out demons. Freely you have received, freely give.

Jesus gave them authority to preach the good news of Messiah during his life on earth. They prayed with people; there were healings; demons were cast out After the Resurrection, Jesus commanded them to preach the good news of his resurrection, salvation through Jesus.

Mark 16: [15] He said to them, "Go into all the world, and preach the gospel to every creature. [16] He who believes and is baptized will be saved. But he who does not believe will be condemned. [17] These signs will accompany those who believe: In My name they will cast out demons; they will speak with new tongues; [18] they will take up serpents; if they drink any deadly thing, it will not hurt them; they will lay hands on the sick, and they will recover."

All of the Apostles served Christ by teaching, preaching, with miracles, signs and wonders following their preaching. The same anointing that was on Jesus for ministry was on the disciples. Afterwards He appointed 70. At Pentecost there were 120. After Pentecost there were over 3, 000 disciples.

Acts 2: [38] Peter said to them, "Repent and be baptized, every one of you, in the name of Jesus Christ for the forgiveness of sins, and you shall receive the gift of the Holy Spirit. [39] For the promise is to you, and to your children, and to all who are far away, as many as the Lord our God will call."

[40] With many other words he testified and exhorted them, saying, "Be saved from this perverse generation." [41] Then those who gladly received his word were baptized, and that day about three thousand souls were added to them.

Mentoring others

Mentors are gifts of God who come along side of your life and willingly offer to train you. As Elijah did with Elisha, the following of the leader is optional to the student. Those who respond by serving the mentor and letting him or her guide their lives, become strong leaders. Mentors can see potential in you and encourage you to live beyond your present norm. They instruct you, encourage you, give you opportunities and help establish you as a leader to live life beyond what you could have imagined on your own. This is the Biblical model.

I myself can credit many people for my past and present success. Teachers, professors mentored me in academics. Pastors, prophets, Apostles, Teachers, Evangelists mentored me in my Christian life. There were some that saw potential in me and gave me opportunities to succeed. In my ministry training studies, Loren Covarubbias, (Mt. Zion Temple) pastor, teacher, prophet, not only taught the classes but encouraged me by choosing me to lead a group of first year students in minister's training school. I myself was learning but was also instructing.

God has put Christian mentors in my life that significantly elevated my position, my responsibilities, my realm of influence using my natural gifts, education, training, as well as Spiritual gifts.

What leaders has God brought into your life to mentor you? Is there one or more? Did you start mentoring someone once you obtained some success?

Mentorship is doing, observing, receiving instruction with a mentor's guidance (John Maxwell). It is a cycle not complete, until the trainee starts mentoring others.

Criteria of a leader

Preparing yourself for ministry

There is necessary heart preparation for ministry. It begins the moment God calls you but, mentors, opportunities, relationship with Christ develop your spiritual fruit as well as your Spiritual gifts. There are strict standards for those to be released in ministry leadership positions within the body of Christ. The standards were not set by denominations or individuals. The main standards for choosing leaders is in the Scriptures.

Reading these scriptures, examining your own heart, praying concerning the scriptures is an excellent way of self preparation for ministry. It is also the way that the Church leadership uses to examine potential leaders.

Most of the criteria is character qualities, spiritual fruit, self-discipline. The emphasis is on moral purity, integrity, maturity.

1 Tim. 3:1 This is a true saying, if a man desire the office of a bishop, he desireth a good work.

²A bishop then must be blameless, the husband of one wife, vigilant, sober, of good behaviour, given to hospitality, apt to teach;

³Not given to wine, no striker, not greedy of filthy lucre; but patient, not a brawler, not covetous;

⁴One that ruleth well his own house, having his children in subjection with all gravity;

⁵(For if a man know not how to rule his own house, how shall he take care of the church of God?)

⁶Not a novice, lest being lifted up with pride he fall into the condemnation of the devil.

⁷Moreover he must have a good report of them which are without; lest he fall into reproach and the snare of the devil.

Self examination without the anointing of the Holy Spirit is merely reflection. Prayerfully examining your heart attitude concerning motivation for ministry is essential. Should you desire promotion in a secular workplace, you should also examine your heart concerning your reasons. Selfishness should never be the main motive for any advancement for a Christian. If you do not desire to sincerely invest in others, serve people, use your talents to assist others, you are seeking the position for selfish reasons. Christian careers are accountable by the standard concerning the scriptures.

Col 3: ²³ And whatever you do, do it heartily, as for the Lord and not for men, ²⁴ knowing that from the Lord you will receive the reward of the inheritance. For you serve the Lord Christ.

God can prosper you, cause you to flourish so that the blessing is upon you. Not only will friends give and serve you but strangers will give, serve you and honour you. It's the blessing of God.

Pray for supernatural favour

It is an excellent prayer to pray over yourself each day – that God would give you supernatural favour with all types of individuals. It is the blessing of God on you that causes people to give you unusual favour. (Deut. 28: 1-14)

Pray for opportunities

God commands us to ask so our joy may be full. (John 16: 24) It means God desires to give us the things we desire (as they align with God's Word), but we must pray, requesting from God. It is not that He doesn't know what we need. He knows but it is our honouring of God to request it and to thank him for the answer. It is honouring God as the source of supply.

John 14: ¹³ I will do whatever you ask in My name, that the Father may be glorified in the Son. ¹⁴ If you ask anything in My name, I will do it. I've prayed for myself concerning all main decisions in my life. God has directed me, prospered me, given the desires of my heart. I know that God is, and He is a rewarder or those who diligently seek Him (Hebrews 11: 6).

Of course, you must prepare yourself with education, training, experience. You must put an effort, but you should also pray that God will give you opportunities each day to magnify Him. Pray over the seasons of your life. Pray over your career, your ministry. God can connect you with someone who can release opportunity to you.

Pray over yourself each day stirring up your gifts, praying that God will use you. As you face each day, expect God to use you. Your words, your actions, your decisions can positively affect the people around you. You can be a life changer by living to your fullest potential.

Obey the promptings of the Holy Spirit

Should you feel a prompting of the Holy Spirit to phone someone or give or serve, you should. A prompting to bless someone is from the Spirit of God. Those gentle nudges on your inner spirit can bless somebody's day. Your phone call can bring hope or encouragement. Your giving can be the answer to someone's prayer. Your life choices in obeying the promptings of the Holy Spirit, determine your success both as a Christian, and as a minister of the gospel. Obeying God's promptings in business can make a difference between success or failure. The Holy Spirit is Christ living in us.

Becoming a Living Word

Scripture is God's Holy Word. It is his plan for us. It is like an operation manual. All products come with instructions. Important products come with a manual. Our lives are so important that God inspired 66 books of the Bible for us. It is the will of God for us – it is God's desire for us to be strong, healthy, prosperous, blessed with abundance. God commands us to get the Word of God on the inside of us. He commands us to believe it, to live it, to teach it to our children, to speak His Word, to write it. It is essential that God's word get into our hearts. God's Word in our hearts means the Word will be our first response. Honouring God's Word is choosing a life of blessing and favour.

Ezekiel 11: [19] I will give them an undivided heart and put a new spirit in them; I will remove from them their heart of stone and give them a heart of flesh. [20] Then they will follow my decrees and be careful to keep my laws. They will be my people, and I will be their God.

Jeremiah 31: [33] "This is the covenant I will make with the people of Israel

after that time," declares the LORD.
"I will put my law in their minds
  and write it on their hearts.
I will be their God,
  and they will be my people.

Deuteronomy 30: [5] See, I set before you today life and prosperity, death and destruction. [16] For I command you today to love the LORD your God, to walk in obedience to him, and to keep his commands, decrees and laws; then you will live and increase, and the LORD your God will bless you in the land you are entering to possess.

Deuteronomy 11: [18] Fix these words of mine in your hearts and minds; tie them as symbols on your hands and bind them on your foreheads. [19] Teach them to your children, talking about them when you sit at home and when you walk along the road, when you lie down and when you get up. [20] Write them on the doorframes of your houses and on your gates, [21] so that your days and the days of your children may be many in the land the LORD swore to give your ancestors, as many as the days that the heavens are above the earth.

Get the Word in you

  Talking about the scriptures is a way of getting the Word into your heart. Saying the scriptures, praying them, posting scripture in your home are all ways of getting the Scriptures into your heart. The more the Word of God is within you, the more you will make decisions based on the Word. God's will for us is a way of life, truth, blessing abundance. Choosing Scripture is choosing God's will for us. It is the best life we could hope to obtain. It is wisdom. It is life.

It would be foolish to get a new car and put sand in the gas tank. It would not be good for the motor. It would cause the car to malfunction. In the same way, sin contaminates a human life – it is the opposite of what God's created us for. It would be wise to study the scriptures, to pray them and to confess them until the Word of God is so deep within our hearts, we become living epistles.

James 1: 21 Wherefore lay apart all filthiness and superfluity of naughtiness, and receive with meekness the engrafted word, which is able to save your souls.

2 Corinthians 3: 2 You yourselves are our letter, written on our hearts, known and read by everyone. 3 You show that you are a letter from Christ, the result of our ministry, written not with ink but with the Spirit of the living God, not on tablets of stone but on tablets of human hearts.

Purpose to live your life on purpose dedicating each part of your day to God. Present yourself as God's servant, each day: spirit, soul and body. It means you yield yourself wholly unto God.

Romans 12: 1 Therefore, I urge you, brothers and sisters, in view of God's mercy, to offer your bodies as a living sacrifice, holy and pleasing to God—this is your true and proper worship. 2 Do not conform to the pattern of this world, but be transformed by the renewing of your mind. Then you will be able to test and approve what God's will is—his good, pleasing and perfect will.

1 Thessalonians 5: 23 May God himself, the God of peace, sanctify you through and through. May your whole spirit, soul and body be kept blameless at the coming of our Lord Jesus Christ.

Sanctify yourself – use communion – covenant to do it

Consecrate yourself unto God each day. Use the communion elements to strengthen yourself in the Spirit. 1 Corinthians 11: 23-31 can be used or words of Christ from the gospels. Worship God wholly; pray for yourself; pray for others. Pray for opportunities where God can use you. Keep presenting yourself to God as available. Expect God to use you. Should you recognize an opportunity – speak what God prompts you to speak. Give. Serve. Encourage. Show mercy. Use your Spiritual gifts and talents.

Chapter end questions

1. Create a list of people who have significantly mentored you impacting your life. Pray for them. Write a card or give a present to them.

2. Create list of people you can sow something into. Create a list of presents that can improve their lives. Create a list of people you can sow into also connect with to start mentoring. Begin it soon.

3. Write some of the ways God has given you divine connections and what the results were. Write occasions you know the supernatural favour of God was on you and the results of it.

7 DESTINY DECISIONS

It is a destiny decision day for many people. There are people making life choices. Students are deciding on programs of study and possible careers. Some are considering marriage. Others are considering buying a new home. Some are considering changing careers. These are all major life decisions. Deciding to yield yourself wholly to God to live the way of Spirit, the way of God's Word is a decision that can impact your life not only for the present but for your eternal future.

Each choice we make leads us to a series of connections and pathways. Some pathways are the best for us. Some are not. Choosing to wholly go the Way to Spirit – is yielding your self wholly to the Holy Spirit. I literally prayed " Holy Spirit be my Senior Partner. Lead and guide me, teach me, anoint me, fill me. Etc." I made a decision. It affected my heart. It affected my words. I prayed" God let your Word be in my heart. Let it be in my mouth. Use my words to add value to people, to speak words of comfort, exhortation, encouragement to others. Holy Spirit correct me if my words don't align with Scripture." Praying this type of radical prayer, means you desire to use you whether it is for mainline ministry or service, workplace excellence, family, community, friends etc.

When you come to a destiny decision, pray. Yield your life to God. Ask God to inspire you. Gloria Copeland stated a way that helped her. I use the method also. It is praying asking for inspiration and then saying "God should I choose this way…" and say it out loud (so you can hear your own voice) in prayer. Expect

God to correct you or confirm the best path for you. Use your wisdom, your education, your training, The Scriptures as a Guide. Make a choice -based on what you believe is best – pray it to God and expect God to direct you. You may feel a check that says "no not that way."

Of course, I am talking about destiny decisions living in righteousness. If you are praying about doing something that directly goes against God's Word, that would be foolish – God's Word is always final authority. God never contradicts His Word. All of us will make destiny decisions on important aspects of our lives. The Holy Spirit is the best Partner because He will direct us in the way that is best for us.

There are occasions God may send someone into your life to confirm the decision choice. Or a mature Christian may speak with you giving you words of wisdom concerning it. There are a multitude of ways God can get a confirmation to you as you pray in consecration. The following passage speaks about Jesus instruction to the disciples to get a colt for him to ride on into Jerusalem on Palm Sunday. The donkey is an ordinary animal. But that day, he was chosen by God for something important.

Jesus rode into Jerusalem with crowds of people waving Palm branches over him crying " Hosanna. Glory to the King". They received him as Messiah. That day is a foreshadow of what yet shall come. Jesus shall return coming into Jerusalem but on the next coming He will come as a triumphant King of kings, Lord of Lords. He will establish His throne in Jerusalem. The colt was chosen that day for a specific purpose – Jesus was going to use it as was prophesied in Zechariah (Zech. 9:9).

Mark 11: ²And saith unto them, Go your way into the village over against you: and as soon as ye be entered into it, ye shall find a colt tied, whereon never man sat; loose him, and bring him.

³And if any man say unto you, Why do ye this? say ye that the Lord hath need of him; and straightway he will send him hither.

⁴And they went their way, and found the colt tied by the door without in a place where two ways met; and they loose him.

⁵And certain of them that stood there said unto them, What do ye, loosing the colt?

⁶And they said unto them even as Jesus had commanded: and they let them go.

The colt that Jesus used to ride into Jerusalem on Palm Sunday was an ordinary donkey until Jesus chose him. It become an extraordinary donkey as it carried Jesus, Messiah through the streets of Jerusalem as people worshipped, waved palm leaves, cried Hosanna!

The colt is between 2 roads or ways. In this scripture an ordinary way/ an extraordinary way. There are many Christians who are in a place of decision making – ordinary life and extraordinary radical Christian life pursuing Christ. Can you relate to the destiny decisions of choices? Christ has need of you. Jesus is calling you to choose to pursue him. Choose the most excellent way – choose the higher way – the way of Spirit – the way of God's Word – Christ desires to use you. Give yourself as a living sacrifice (Rom 12: 1-2). Say yes to Jesus – obey the promptings of the Holy Spirit. Receive the word – Christ desires you – wants to use you. Commit yourself wholly spirit soul body (1 Thess. 5: 23)– spirit soul body – consecrate yourself as a servant minister for Christ. That means you will obey the promptings of the Holy Spirit

– you will speak, preach, share Christ with others as God directs you. Yield your life to the Holy Spirit so that God may direct your paths. You may be released in ministry (apostles prophet evangelist pastor teacher) or in your sphere of authority as a light for Christ. Whatever way – God directs you. Expect God to direct you. You will not forget God's guidance, nor will you ever regret it. Should you choose the highest way, the way of Spirit, the way of God's Word – you are choosing the most excellent way. Your life will be blessed in all you do.

Life destiny decisions you are facing could be school, career, marriage, decisions that effect your life on earth – life long commitments or eternal choices such ministry decisions that will impact your life an earth also your eternal rewards.

Scriptural Examples of Destiny Decisions

JOSHUA – BLESSED BY MOSES – ANOINTED BY GOD – SPEAKS OVER ISRAEL - A DAY OF DECISION
Joshua - Choose ye this day

Joshua was with Moses on Mt. Sinai. He was assistant to Moses through the wilderness. Joshua and Caleb had a good report. They believed God could grant Israel the victory that Israel could inherit the land. Joshua was sentenced along with Moses and the believing Jews to be in the wilderness with the unbelieving Israelites years even though he believed God. The majority of the Israelites did not receive the report of Joshua or Caleb who suggested they immediately go in and possess the land God had promised. It was a lush rich land with huge fruit and with streams. It was as God had promised. The majority believed the foolish spies who did not believe God could give them the promised land because there were strong inhabitants of the land.

Joshua was blessed – His faith in God was his strength. He honoured God, served Moses and Israel all his life. Joshua knew the miracles of Egypt was a witness of God's deliverance of Israel. Joshua believed God with his life. At the age of 80 he was entering into the land God had promised him.

Moses anointed Joshua to be the next leader so that Israel would know that Joshua was chosen by God and also so they could see Moses approval, impartation on Joshua so Israel would obey him. He was God's Chosen leader.

Deuteronomy 31: [7] Then Moses summoned Joshua and said to him in the presence of all Israel, "Be strong and courageous, for you must go with this people into the land that the LORD swore to their ancestors to give them, and you must divide it among them as their inheritance. [8] The LORD himself goes before you and will be with you; he will never leave you nor forsake you. Do not be afraid; do not be discouraged."

God kept nothing from his servant Moses concerning the future of Israel. He let Moses know that Israel would serve idols and turn from God. This would have grieved Moses as it grieved God. It was a way that God could warn Israel of the consequences.

It was a way that Moses through Joshua could continue interceding for Israel.

Deuteronomy 31: [14] The LORD said to Moses, "Now the day of your death is near. Call Joshua and present yourselves at the tent of meeting, where I will commission him." So Moses and Joshua came and presented themselves at the tent of meeting.

[15] Then the LORD appeared at the tent in a pillar of cloud, and the cloud stood over the entrance to the tent. [16] And the LORD said to Moses: "You are going to rest with your ancestors, and these people will soon prostitute themselves to the foreign gods of the land they are entering. They will forsake me and break the covenant I made with them. [17] And in that day I will become angry with them and forsake them; I will hide my face from them, and they will be destroyed. Many disasters and calamities will come on them, and in that day they will ask, 'Have not these disasters come on us because our God is not with us?' [18] And I will certainly hide my face in that day because of all their wickedness in turning to other gods.

After Israel inherited the land, Joshua warned the people to obey God and not turn away. Joshua knew Israel would abandon God's ways so he warned them. Because God's heart is for Israel to worship Him so He can bless them, He warned them what could occur should they abandon God. It could lead them to repentance. It was the mercy of God warning Israel. Joshua spoke profound words often quoted by Christians " As for me and mine, we will serve the LORD." Joshua made his decision to serve God before entering the land. Fixing his heart, his values on God –

realizing the only way is God's way – the way of the blessing, was his declaration.

Joshua 24: [14] "Now fear the LORD and serve him with all faithfulness. Throw away the gods your ancestors worshiped beyond the Euphrates River and in Egypt, and serve the LORD. [15] But if serving the LORD seems undesirable to you, then choose for yourselves this day whom you will serve, whether the gods your ancestors served beyond the Euphrates, or the gods of the Amorites, in whose land you are living. But as for me and my household, we will serve the LORD."

Thomas – Didymus – doubting – believing – opposites

Thomas Didymus name definition means opposing yourself or divided self. A self divided is in constant war within itself. This is an unconverted soul, not yet a believer in Jesus. It was his was education, logical thinking vs faith. He believed only what he could sense with his senses. There are many philosophers who believe the same way. If you can't sense it, it isn't true or real. But this is absurd concerning all modern-day technology. This is absurd concerning faith. Faith is the substance of things hoped for, the evidence of things not yet seen (Hebrews 11:1). Hope is the vital ingredient that leads us to believe God's Word. It results in faith – believing that God is – and is a rewarder of those who diligently seek Him.

Thomas heard the stories of the disciples who encountered the resurrected Jesus. He wanted to believe but doubted without physical evidence the resurrection of Christ. He would not believe unless... His natural course was unbelief without proof. Secular life. This is the same as non- Christians, but Thomas had lived with Jesus, seen the miracles, heard the preaching, yet he did not believe.

A Christian living a life of faith believes – receives – possesses – obtains – the blessings because they believe God's Word. God set His Word above his name. His Word is the highest authority. God's promises are for us who believe in Jesus Christ. We inherit the blessings of Israel through Jesus Christ – the blessings of the Abrahamic Covenant, the blessings of the Mosaic covenant – are ours because of Jesus shed blood.

Although Thomas would not believe without physical proof, Jesus, showed mercy on him – appeared within the room without going through a physical door– saying the exact words of Thomas that no one would know except God and the disciples Thomas spoke. Jesus was providing proof that He was God.

Jesus offered proof of his wounds – even saying that Thomas could put his fingers through the nail wounds in his bones. Thomas responded with faith. He had seen, he believed. He immediately calls Jesus "My Lord and

My God". Jesus blesses him but says it is best for those who can believe without doubting – without seeing. The truth here is that God would encourage us to believe scripture without physical proof. Faith in the word of God brings results. But there are some who will not believe until they get physical proof. Rather than rebuke and dismiss him, Jesus provides the proof. In Pentecostal, Charismatic, four square, full gospel churches, we should believe the Word of God, pray it receive it.

There is the same type of unbelief evident in Gideon (Genesis 6: 36-40). Gideon asked God to prove his conversation with Gideon instructing him to lead the army by placing a fleece (lamb's wool) it would get soaking wet but the ground would be dry. It occurred. The next day Gideon asked that the fleece be dry and the ground be all wet. It occurred. Gideon got boldness because of the proof and obeyed God.

John 20 : [24] Now Thomas (also known as Didymus[a]), one of the Twelve, was not with the disciples when Jesus came. [25] So the other disciples told him, "We have seen the Lord!"

But he said to them, "Unless I see the nail marks in his hands and put my finger where the nails were, and put my hand into his side, I will not believe."

[26] A week later his disciples were in the house again, and Thomas was with them. Though the doors were locked, Jesus came and stood among them and said, "Peace be with you!" [27] Then he said

to Thomas, "Put your finger here; see my hands. Reach out your hand and put it into my side. Stop doubting and believe."

[28] Thomas said to him, "My Lord and my God!"

[29] Then Jesus told him, "Because you have seen me, you have believed; blessed are those who have not seen and yet have believed."

Faith Believes God's Word

Believing in the Scriptures without physical proof is the highest form of faith. It means you believe because God said so. Faith comes by hearing and hearing by the Word of God (Romans 10: 17). Faith comes by listening to the Word of God, reading the Word of God, praying the Word of God, confessing the word of God. Get the Word of God on the inside of you, you will be believing not doubting.

Choose one way - Christ

Although there may be choices, choose the way of faith. Choose the direction that would be God's best for your life. It would mean praying. It may be that someone comes into your life and releases you with words encouraging you to use your gifts and potential, to dream and to take steps towards obtaining it. It is my intention that this book would encourage you, release you to aim for the highest potential of your life so you can achieve for Christ. Should you obtain success, you will train others; sow into other's lives causing them to train others.

Should you feel divided in a place of decision, you can be released into ministry – words of wisdom from a friend, pastor or leader – can release someone to make a wise choice someone must release them – prophets and apostles can release people into their destiny by recognizing the calling of God on a person. Go to your respected mentors and leaders first. Should there not be someone right now, go to a prophetic conference expecting to hear from God. You can fast and pray at home. Go without food or certain types of food on purpose while you pray about your situation. Expect God to speak to you – He will. He can give you a dream; He can give you an impression; He can quicken a scripture to you. God can make it clear to you the best path for you. Desire God more than the decision, the answer will be released.

Should you feel a prompting to encourage someone to use his or her giftings, be in obedience to speak the words – encouragement, exhortation, comfort – God can inspire you to speak words to someone that would radically impact his or her life. Your simple obedience may be one of the confirmations a person is praying for.

Pray that God may use you to encourage others so they can be used by God in their gifts and talents. Pray for others for Divine connections and Supernatural favour. It is truly loving others as you would your own self.

This point in your life

You are reading this book, it is not a coincidence. It is a call to radical Christian life. It is saying yes to extraordinary life. It is saying yes to Christ. What is your dream? What are the steps to get you there? What practical things can you do to prepare to achieve your dream. Is it necessary to obtain higher education? Is it necessary to receive mentorship? What things are necessary?

Make a list of necessary things. Write a plan of how long it could take to achieve these things naturally. Get yourself what is necessary. Get training, education, ministry experience, humility, godly character, godly fruit. Choose a self improvement plan, a development plan to help you achieve your goals.
Write your goals 1) for the next year 2) next 5 years 3) next 10 years

What would or should you do to get there? Make a long list of necessary practical things you can do to get there.

Your career choice should be your passion. You should enjoy it more than anything. If it seems that you are doing a job you hate, you should get training, education, mentorship to obtain the position you would enjoy doing.

Create a plan to achieving it. Yearly. Monthly – keep moving towards your plan.

Your dream – goal – for ministry or for career as well as ministry is worth pursuing. Invest in resources that can help you achieve your goals. I recommend Maxwell's books (Dream Map , Put your dream to the Test). Create a practical plan of goals to reach – 1 year or more – or as long as it takes –thorough examination of your own dreams in specific ways. It will cause you to formulate an intricate, detailed list of practical things you can do in achieving the dream plan. Do all you can do yourself. Pray for divine connections. Pray for supernatural favour. Start sowing into others' lives; get mentorship and start mentoring others. The release into your destiny will come as you are pursuing it doing these things. God can put someone in your life who can introduce you to your next boss. God can put someone in your life that can introduce you to your spouse to be. There is the supernatural favour of God element that comes to you as a covenant believer.

End of Chapter questions

1. What are your dreams for your future? Career? Ministry?

2. Write a list of successful people who you could learn from to obtain your goal.

3. Write a list of questions you could speak to those people to get you to your desired goal.

8 THE SELECTION

The day you are selected is a special day. Ideally it means you've studied, you've prepared yourself, you've got some education, experience in ministry, your character is Christlike. You are ready for an assignment. Should you think your ready, it doesn't mean you are. You can believe you are ready, but until you are performing in your career or ministry opportunity, you won't know. Should you be wholly consecrated to God and chosen, yes you are ready, or you wouldn't get the invitation. You may be deciding between 2 or more opportunities. There was an excellent American missionary Sam Sasser, who preached in the South Pacific. One of his many books is on vessels that God creates and making yourself ready for God to use. The chosen vessel is of particular importance as it is often left on a high shelf long because its use is so specific and unusual. It is beautiful, excellent – yet most people do not choose it. Most people choose vessels for everyday use. The chosen vessel is for a specific purpose – a Divine use.

2 Timothy 2: [20] In a large house there are articles not only of gold and silver, but also of wood and clay; some are for special purposes and some for common use. [21] Those who cleanse themselves from the latter will be instruments for special purposes, made holy, useful to the Master and prepared to do any good work.

Should you be one of those who choose to live a life of radical obedience to Christ, wholly submitting to the Holy Spirit – you are not usual – you are peculiar – specific – extraordinary – because of Christ who lives within you. Those with education, experience, character, willingness etc. are different. You realize the fruit of your life can impact beyond your years. You sow your life into Christ so you can reap a harvest after your life. You purposely train others, invest in Christian ministries, your church, your workplace, your community. Invest with your life, your prayer as well as your finances, You may leave financial tributes to those as well as others. It is knowing that there is a reason for your life. It is knowing there is more than simply this life in the importance of decisions.

Your life potential is ready. What occurs next is a Divine connection. It is the calling. It is an opportunity that lets you use your education and training. It is a ministry opportunity that lets you use your Spiritual gifts, talents, abilities. It is a beginning.

Section 3

1 Kings 19- [19] So he departed thence, and found Elisha the son of Shaphat, who was plowing with twelve yoke of oxen before him, and he with the twelfth: and Elijah passed by him, and cast his mantle upon him.

[20] And he left the oxen, and ran after Elijah, and said, Let me, I pray thee, kiss my father and my mother, and then I will follow thee. And he said unto him, Go back again: for what have I done to thee?

²¹And he returned back from him, and took a yoke of oxen, and slew them, and boiled their flesh with the instruments of the oxen, and gave unto the people, and they did eat. Then he arose, and went after Elijah, and ministered unto him.

Elijah was instructed by God to anoint Elisha as a prophet and to tarin him for ministry as a prophet. He cast his mantle on Elisha that was his identity as a prophet. He was inviting Elisha to leave his ordinary life to pursue life with God. Elisha's first response was to run after Elijah but he wanted to kiss his parents and conclude his ordinary life. He did. He slew the 12 oxen – his means of living in his ordinary life – and followed Elijah. His life was radically changed. Rather than routine tasks, his life became ministering miracles and assisting Elijah with his role as Prophet of Israel.

The day of your calling is a new beginning. It is as though your investment in yourself serving Christ is now at a place where you can begin to train others. You will be in a position to serve, learn from others in a new environment. You will be in a position to train others. Once someone has taught you, trained you, you must continue to train others. It is essential. God's kingdom is built on giving, serving, sowing spiritually into others. Once you have received training and some success, start mentoring others.

There are some who will especially dedicate their lives to a career, with some ministry service. There will be others who especially dedicate themselves to Christian Ministry service with some secular connections. There are some who wholly serve in both. There are not as many who successfully serve wholly in career as well as in church. There are some though. It is a special type of person who serves God through his or her career as well as serves Christ in his or her church. It is realizing your life is a gift from God and the best gift you can give to God is your life. Keep excellence in the workplace. Keep excellence in the ministry.

The Apostle Paul is an example of this type of excellence. He worked as a tentmaker. He was an expert in the Torah, a Pharisee, most excellent in his education, Greek, Hebrew, Latin. He was passionate, zealous. Until he encountered Christ on the Damascus road, he was not fulfilling his purpose. After he met Christ, he was released into his purpose. He worked so he could minister. He supported himself. He was determined to preach the gospel – and could get money by using his talents so he did.

2 Timothy 2: [9] Surely you remember, brothers and sisters, our toil and hardship; we worked night and day in order not to be a burden to anyone while we preached the gospel of God to you. [10] You are witnesses, and so is God, of how holy, righteous and blameless we were among you who believed. [11] For you know that we dealt with each of you as a father deals with his own children, [12] encouraging, comforting and urging you to live lives worthy of God, who calls you into his kingdom and glory.

2 Corinthians 11: [9] And when I was with you and needed something, I was not a burden to anyone, for the brothers who came from Macedonia supplied what I needed. I have kept myself from being a burden to you in any way, and will continue to do so.

There are some who will serve both in the Church, as well as the profession during their lives. Should you not be in ministry only, it is the goal you should aim for as a Christian – you should be serving also in the Church. There is no such thing as those not called to ministry. There are some only called to the five- fold ministry: Apostles, Prophets, Pastors, Teachers, Evangelists. But there are some who will hold positions of authority in the Church as well as in their profession/career.

You are a Christian, you should be serving in the Church, in missions, in Christian organizations. All people should be serving in some capacity within their spheres of influence. Not all have the same callings – but all Christians are called to minister in some way. All the body of Christ have Spiritual gifts. There is a purpose for you beyond your job or career. You are to use your giftings in some way within the Body of Christ. You may teach Sunday school, teach a Bible class, serve as an usher, greeter, deacon or elder. You may be a youth leader. You could be cooking or cleaning in the Church. There is a place for everyone. There is something you will do in the Church that you excel at that you can do excellently making a difference. You will know it is what you should be doing. It fits like a hand in a glove. You know it is your calling. Not all are to preach from the pulpit. Some are – some are not. You will know immediately if it is not what you were meant to do. I discuss this topic in much more detail in my book on Spiritual Gifts also in my book Living Life Fully. Start serving in some way within your Church. Should opportunities come for you with missionary organizations, pray about them seriously rather than not take them.

Should you be using your gifts in the career, it most certainly is essentially important, but it is necessary that you contribute in some way within the Body of Christ. Those who are in ministry in the Church should be contributing to their communities in some way. They could coach sports, be involved in their children's schools, committees or volunteer within the community in some way. There should be some contribution to the Community. It could be a connection through the church such as a feeding program in the schools or the giving by a Church to a food bank. Many churches contribute to the community as an organized Community event. My own Church sponsors special events to invite the community. There are concerts, dramas, a type of fun day Christian carnival with games, clowns, rides for children etc. It is an excellent way of evangelizing. It is important that ministers, mature Christians get experience with people who are new Christians or pre-Christians. It is a chance for God to shine the light of His glory through us to those who may never get a chance to know God any other way.

Matthew 5: [14] "You are the light of the world. A town built on a hill cannot be hidden. [15] Neither do people light a lamp and put it under a bowl. Instead they put it on its stand, and it gives light to everyone in the house. [16] In the same way, let your light shine before others, that they may see your good deeds and glorify your Father in heaven.

In your life at present write where you are in your life. Is it on a road to a Career? Is it a way of ministry in the Church?

What occurred first? Christians have the privilege and honour to serve God in the Church as soon as they are children. Teens can contribute in Church. Often youth serve with passion and zeal because of their energy. Is there a mentor in your life now? Are there respected people you can speak with that can point you towards your goals in Church? in a Career? Make a list of them.

Plan to approach them. Create a list of questions to ask them. When you meet with them, bring paper and pen or a voice recorder so you can get the best from your discussion.

Sample questions can be as follows: What studies did you take in school to obtain your position? Did you feel the direction of God in your decision making? What mentors trained you? How did they make a difference in your life?

1. Write a concise sentence or paragraph defining your career goal.
2. Write a concise sentence or paragraph that defines your ministry goals.
3. Write a paragraph that describes your plan to achieving these goals.

As you trust the mentor, share your personal plans with them asking for input, direction. Ask the person(s) if he/she has concerns regarding your plans.

Add your own questions. These are only sample questions. Prepare to listen to their life stories of inspiration and learn what you can from their words.

You can write your goals for these topics but realize since it involves someone else's will, the results may vary.

Family – Aim to have an excellent member with each of them.
Marriage – Should you desire it, at what point would you get married?
Children – Do you want children? Is it important?
Relationships – your closest friendships – aim to have an excellent relationship with each of them.
Those you mentor - purposely sow into their lives so they use their gifts and talents.
Those who mentor you – respect them, seriously listen to them. Be careful of the length of your discussions. It would be wise to ask for 1 hour and stick to the duration. Do not worship them. Respect them. Honour them. Realize God has blessed them. Receive what you can. Always be considerate. You can give them presents or notes or appreciation cards. Your success is what a true mentor wants for you. Share your success and remember those who helped you achieve it.

Romans 13: [7] Render therefore to all their dues: tribute to whom tribute is due; custom to whom custom; fear to whom fear; honour to whom honour.

Bible Discipleship – Mentoring

Elisha was chosen to serve Elijah. That doesn't seem much of a calling. But his being with Elijah for that season of his life meant he learned the character of a Prophet of God, the integrity of the prophet of God, the mantle of Elijah – or the calling. He learned the calling of himself through being with Elijah. True mentorship occurred. The mantle was to be passed on but it had to be earned. It can only come the way of the Spirit, the way of the Scriptures.

The Mantle

The mantle of Elijah was his obedience to speak the words of God to those God commanded. His calling was as Prophet over Israel. He served his nation during his life with such excellence his exit from earth was unusual. He spoke tough words to kings that would not obey God unless miracles manifested. He spoke kind words to those who begged him for miracles. He served God by serving the people of Israel but honouring only God. He was God's mouth in Israel. Ahab hated him but feared him because Elijah spoke the truth of the sins of Israel. Jezebel, the queen hated him and wanted to kill him. She hired people to kill him. There are many miracles discussed in scripture including the resurrection of the death. One of his greatest victories was at Mt. Carmel.

Elijah challenged the prophets of Baal to a miracle show down. His challenge was not only to them but all of Israel who gathered to watch the spectacle. Elijah would make an altar to God, get the wood. The prophets of Baal got the wood and made an altar to their God. The God who would consume the sacrifice with fire – was to be declared the true God.

1 Kings 18: [22] Then Elijah said to them, "I am the only one of the LORD's prophets left, but Baal has four hundred and fifty prophets. [23] Get two bulls for us. Let Baal's prophets choose one for themselves, and let them cut it into pieces and put it on the wood but not set fire to it. I will prepare the other bull and put it on the wood but not set fire to it. [24] Then you call on the name of your god, and I will call on the name of the LORD. The god who answers by fire—he is God."

The prophets of Baal cut themselves, offering their blood trying to get the fire started. There was no response.

[25] Elijah said to the prophets of Baal, "Choose one of the bulls and prepare it first, since there are so many of you. Call on the name of your god, but do not light the fire." [26] So they took the bull given them and prepared it.

Then they called on the name of Baal from morning till noon. "Baal, answer us!" they shouted. But there was no response; no one answered. And they danced around the altar they had made.

[27] At noon Elijah began to taunt them. "Shout louder!" he said. "Surely he is a god! Perhaps he is deep in thought, or busy, or traveling. Maybe he is sleeping and must be awakened." [28] So they shouted louder and slashed themselves with swords and spears, as was their custom, until their blood flowed. [29] Midday passed, and they continued their frantic prophesying until the time for the

evening sacrifice. But there was no response, no one answered, no one paid attention.

Even though they offered their life's blood, Baal could not respond because he is no god. The God of Israel Jehovah would not allow any demon to manifest that day. Elijah repaired the altar of the Lord. Elijah prepared the offering. The God of Israel manifested his glory so that all who witnessed it knew He was God. Elijah had water poured over the wood so there was no physical way the fire could start. Elijah prayed. God consumed the sacrifice with a blaze of fire.

1 Kings 18: [30] Then Elijah said to all the people, "Come here to me." They came to him, and he repaired the altar of the LORD, which had been torn down. [31] Elijah took twelve stones, one for each of the tribes descended from Jacob, to whom the word of the LORD had come, saying, "Your name shall be Israel." [32] With the stones he built an altar in the name of the LORD, and he dug a trench around it large enough to hold two seahs[a] of seed. [33] He arranged the wood, cut the bull into pieces and laid it on the wood. Then he said to them, "Fill four large jars with water and pour it on the offering and on the wood."

[34] "Do it again," he said, and they did it again.

"Do it a third time," he ordered, and they did it the third time. [35] The water ran down around the altar and even filled the trench.

[36] At the time of sacrifice, the prophet Elijah stepped forward and prayed: "LORD, the God of Abraham, Isaac and Israel, let it be

known today that you are God in Israel and that I am your servant and have done all these things at your command. ³⁷ Answer me, LORD, answer me, so these people will know that you, LORD, are God, and that you are turning their hearts back again."

³⁸ Then the fire of the LORD fell and burned up the sacrifice, the wood, the stones and the soil, and also licked up the water in the trench.

³⁹ When all the people saw this, they fell prostrate and cried, "The LORD—he is God! The LORD—he is God!"

Once all of Israel knew the truth of the God of Israel they obeyed Elijah. Elijah slew 500 prophets of Baal that day.

⁴⁰ Then Elijah commanded them, "Seize the prophets of Baal. Don't let anyone get away!" They seized them, and Elijah had them brought down to the Kishon Valley and slaughtered there.

Afterwards, the drought that Israel had experience for years, ended. There was rain. The prophet Elijah prayed for the rain. It rained.

This was a magnificent victory for Jehovah God as well as the prophet Elijah. Jezebel, was filled with hatred and commanded her people to kill Elijah. Elijah ran for his life.

1 Kings 19: 1 Now Ahab told Jezebel everything Elijah had done and how he had killed all the prophets with the sword. ² So Jezebel sent a messenger to Elijah to say, "May the gods deal with

me, be it ever so severely, if by this time tomorrow I do not make your life like that of one of them."

God sent an angel to give refreshment of food and water to Elijah. He was told to go to Mt Horeb. His instructions from God were complete. Elijah was weary but he obeyed God. It took him 40 days to get to Horeb. It was there God gave him direction to anoint others for ministry. God chose Elisha. Elijah was prophet over spheres of authority impacting the king of Israel, the king of Syria, and the new prophet of Israel. It was at the entrance of the cave that God spoke to Elijah.

Elijah wrapped his face in his mantle

The mantle was the authority of God – the anointing on Elijah for his ministry as a Prophet. The physical mantle he wore was symbolic of it. In itself, it was ordinary clothing. With the anointing of God upon Elijah it was hid identity. He wrapped his face in his mantle is his total embracing of his identity as a prophet of God. It is his calling from God that brought him to the cave in obedience to the angel. It was the calling of God that allowed him to kill 500 prophets of Baal. Because he honoured God wholly during his life, God spoke to him with special instruction. Elijah confessed the situation as he felt it. It was not the whole reality. He had been threatened and they were trying to kill him. He confessed what he had experienced, yet he did not have revelation of the whole picture. God explained the true situation to him. God lifted the burden from him by designating others to carry the responsibility of Israel. God explained how each of the people Elijah would anoint would help to defeat Ahab and Jezebel. From

God's words, Elijah was strengthened. His next task was to anoint the people with God's blessing, calling to ministry.

1 KINGS 19: [13] And it was so, when Elijah heard it, that he wrapped his face in his mantle, and went out, and stood in the entering in of the cave. And, behold, there came a voice unto him, and said, What do'est thou here, Elijah?

[14] And he said, I have been very jealous for the LORD God of hosts: because the children of Israel have forsaken thy covenant, thrown down thine altars, and slain thy prophets with the sword; and I, even I only, am left; and they seek my life, to take it away.

[15] And the LORD said unto him, Go, return on thy way to the wilderness of Damascus: and when thou comest, anoint Hazael to be king over Syria:

[16] And Jehu the son of Nimshi shalt thou anoint to be king over Israel: and Elisha the son of Shaphat of Abelmeholah shalt thou anoint to be prophet in thy room.

[17] And it shall come to pass, that him that escapeth the sword of Hazael shall Jehu slay: and him that escapeth from the sword of Jehu shall Elisha slay.

Elijah was given specific instructions about whom to anoint. Jehu would fight against the false gods and their prophets. He would oppose Ahab and Jezebel. Hazel as King of Syria was a God ordained position meaning he would oppose false gods. It was from there Elisha was next chosen to receive the mantle of Elijah.

As the mantle was cast upon Elisha, he spoke with Elijah running after him. He knew what it meant but wanted to end his old life by greeting his parents and completing his tasks. Elisha went back to say bye to his parents. He was sincere. He slew the oxen – his livelihood. He gave it away. He went after Elijah and ministered to him. He was known as one who washed the hands of Elijah.

SERVING THE ANOINTED PROPHET

His minor role as a servant to Elijah was most significant because it is by the day to day living with someone, that true discipleship occurs. It is not only in the major celebratory events that discipleship occurs. They are not unimportant victories, but it is the daily lifestyle of serving God, honouring God, keeping His Word, preaching it, living it that true integrity can be witnessed. Living with a person is the best way to comprehend the person. Elisha learned the character of Elijah and it gave him boldness for ministry.

Elijah's departure

There are 2 individuals who ascended into heaven without a physical death. Jesus Christ would be the third who ascended into heaven - but he died, rose from the dead, appeared 40 days, then ascended. Enoch was on the earth and then was translated (went directly to heaven without physical death). Elijah had a magnificent homegoing – I mean his leaving of the earth and departure into heaven visibly. God could have done it in many ways. The tribute God gave to Elijah was with glory, supernatural manifestation and honour for his excellent service all his life.

2 Kings 2:1 And it came to pass, when the Lord would take up Elijah into heaven by a whirlwind, that Elijah went with Elisha from Gilgal. Elijah knew he would depart the earth. The conversation is not recorded in scripture, but Elijah knew he would go. Seemingly so did Elisha know that Elijah would depart from the earth. All the prophets of Israel knew that Elijah would depart from the earth. Somehow Elisha knew he should stay with his master and not let him go anywhere without him.

In 2 Kings 2, Elijah went with Elisha from Gilgal. It was spoken at each of the places he visited. Prophets prophesied Elijah's homegoing to Elisha. Elisha responded the same each occasion. He said he knew it was true. At each of these places the sons of the prophets said to Elisha "Do you know the Lord is going to take Elijah away from you today?

At each spot Elijah asked Elisha to stay in the place. Elisha would not leave his master. He knew it was essential to his destiny.

Bethel vs 2 And Elisha said unto him, As the Lord liveth, and as thy soul liveth, I will not leave thee.
Jerico vs 4 5 And the sons of the prophets that were at Jericho came to Elisha, and said unto him, Knowest thou that the Lord will take away thy master from thy head to day? And he answered, Yea, I know it; hold ye your peace.

Jordan vs 6

It was at the Jordan River that the last request of Elijah to Elisha to remain behind occurred. Because he would not stay, Elisha was witness to a miracle. Elijah took his mantle and stuck the waters and they separated. The mantle represented the authority of the God of Israel. The priests of Israel had stepped into the waters of this Jordan with the Ark of the Covenant as Israel the people entered the promised land. The waters were separated. Israel walked into Jordan on dry ground. Elijah and Elisha walked through the midst of the Jordan on dry ground. It was a display of God's glory but it was significant also because it represented the Covenant God made with Israel through Moses and the inheritance of Israel by the leading of Joshua. All the glory was to the God of Israel.

2 Kings 2: ⁶ And Elijah said unto him, Tarry, I pray thee, here; for the LORD hath sent me to Jordan. And he said, As the LORD liveth, and as thy soul liveth, I will not leave thee. And they two went on.

⁷ And fifty men of the sons of the prophets went, and stood to view afar off: and they two stood by Jordan.

⁸ And Elijah took his mantle, and wrapped it together, and smote the waters, and they were divided hither and thither, so that they two went over on dry ground.

It is after this miracle that Elijah asks Elisha what he wanted. Elisha had boldness. He didn't ask for an anointing but more than an anointing a double portion anointing upon his life. Elijah instructed him saying it was a tough thing, but it could occur should he witness Elijah's departure.

2 Kings 2: [9] And it came to pass, when they were gone over, that Elijah said unto Elisha, Ask what I shall do for thee, before I be taken away from thee. And Elisha said, I pray thee, let a double portion of thy spirit be upon me.

[10] And he said, Thou hast asked a hard thing: nevertheless, if thou see me when I am taken from thee, it shall be so unto thee; but if not, it shall not be so.

As they continued walking and talking, Elisha witnessed the next miracle. A chariot of fire with horses of fire appeared. They appeared as fire, but they were not fire. It was a spiritual manifestation of the glory of God. Chariots would be ridden by commanders of armies or kings. God had prepared a chariot for Elijah. Elijah was taken up into the air by a whirlwind and placed into the chariot. It was from this spot in the air – in the midst of his transition to heaven, he released his mantle to Elisha.

2 Kings 2: [11] And it came to pass, as they still went on, and talked, that, behold, there appeared a chariot of fire, and horses of fire, and parted them both asunder; and Elijah went up by a whirlwind into heaven.

Elisha responded with both joy, amazement and awe as he saw it occur. He realized the thing he had asked would be his because he was witnessing the miracle. The tearing of his clothes is a Jewish tradition of mourning. He knew his earthly mentor was no longer there. He knew it meant a new life for him, but he loved his master.

¹² And Elisha saw it, and he cried, My father, my father, the chariot of Israel, and the horsemen thereof. And he saw him no more: and he took hold of his own clothes, and rent them in two pieces.

With boldness, he took up the mantle and struck the waters of the Jordan. He cried out "Where is the God of Elijah?" He was commanding the waters to part – as he saw his master hit the waters with his mantle. The anointing of Elijah was on Elisha. The waters parted.

¹³ He took up also the mantle of Elijah that fell from him, and went back, and stood by the bank of Jordan;

¹⁴ And he took the mantle of Elijah that fell from him, and smote the waters, and said, Where is the LORD God of Elijah? and when he also had smitten the waters, they parted hither and thither: and Elisha went over.

He was not the only witness of this miracle. There were prophets who witnessed it occur. They knew the anointing was on Elisha.

¹⁵ And when the sons of the prophets which were to view at Jericho saw him, they said, The spirit of Elijah doth rest on Elisha. And they came to meet him, and bowed themselves to the ground before him.

The anointing on your life will be witnessed by more than one person. People will recognize the anointing on you. They will come to you expecting God to use you. The anointing is attractive. It draws people to you. It causes them to respect your authority in a sphere of influence in their lives. It may be your success in your workplace, or it may be your promotion or ordination in Church. It is beyond your natural talent. It is God's empowering presence upon your life to effectively excel at whatever you do. It is the blessing of the Mosaic covenant but also the anointing is specific to your calling. You can excel at your calling. It is your joy. It is your passion; it is your success.

Chapter End Questions

1. Did you experience a calling for ministry inwardly in your spirit?
2. Did you experience a leading by God towards your career?
3. List the people who mentored you, (directly affected you) encouraged you, (some positive impact) cheered you on (on the sidelines but positive).

9 MENTORING

Being mentored by someone means spending time with him or her. He or she will speak directly to you about your strengths and areas of weakness. He or she will recognize your character qualities, your potential. He or she will directly give you resources such as books, Cds, conference entry or other such things to sow into your life so you are improving in your areas of strength. Mentors invest in your life with true parent like concern. They invest hours with you. Because they are successful themselves, they can share things with you, so you avoid errors. Giving of their hours with you is a sacrifice because they are extremely busy, successful, involved. The fact they are investing in you means they are investing in others also. They probably volunteer as well as work.

A true mentor will remain with you over your life, but the relationship will evolve. There are excellent resources on mentoring. I highly recommend John Maxwell's training books, Cds, his company of team experts. He lives the very thing I am speaking of and trains millions of people. It is essential that you also keep investing in others. You should use your successes to train others to be successful. Maxwell's book on "Living Life Intentionally" is an excellent resource to begin your self-improvement with.

PROPHECY AND SPECIAL WORDS OF ENCOURAGEMENT
OWNING THEM

Should you receive special words of encouragement from your mentors or leaders, should you receive personal prophecies concerning your life, you should document them – write them in a book. You should reread them, pray about them and embrace them. Often those mentors or leaders that train you, will get revelation from God of your strengths and areas to develop. They may caution you about other areas also. These things should be added to your own list of your personal strengths. You should write a list of all your strengths. They should be areas you invest most of your efforts improving in your areas of strength. This is your area of expertise. These strengths can boost you in the workplace or in ministry. As in all types of coaching, the athlete should listen to the coach; an excellent coach will cause you to achieve beyond what you could have thought was possible. Should you ignore the coach, you will never obtain your full potential. Mentorship is relationship. There is giving and receiving. You are mostly receiving at first, but as you get stronger in your areas of expertise, you may assist your mentor. It becomes synergy. He or she adds value to you; you add value to he or she.

Owning your prophecies or special words of encouragement means you agree, you apply these things, you make efforts to improve in your life in those areas. It means you self-invest, by purchasing books, cds etc. to improve yourself. Lifelong learning with a personal growth plan means you are learning, serving, giving, training others. Receiving only and never investing in others will never get you true success as I am speaking of. True success is living life to please God, serving others, giving, caring as though it is for your own self.

Mark 12: [29] And Jesus answered him, The first of all the commandments is, Hear, O Israel; The Lord our God is one Lord:

[30] And thou shalt love the Lord thy God with all thy heart, and with all thy soul, and with all thy mind, and with all thy strength: this is the first commandment.

[31] And the second is like, namely this, Thou shalt love thy neighbour as thyself. There is none other commandment greater than these.

Living to your potential means you are constantly improving; you are constantly training others. It is a life of fulfillment. The reward is pleasing God. The reward is giving to others and taking joy in others' success as though it were your own. The Apostle Paul encouraged Timothy who he had trained to remember the prophetic words and to hold on to them. Truly the words of special wisdom given by leaders in your life should not be ignored. They can be a catalyst to your achieving your dreams and beyond what you could have imagined.

1 TIMOTHY 1:18

This charge do I commit unto thee son Timothy according to the prophecies which went before on them that thou by them that thou by them mightiest war a good warfare.
Vs 19 holding faith and a good conscience...

The Apostle Paul also gives a word of caution to keep the faith. It means your spiritual life must always be your first priority. Christ is the main reason for life. All we do is as unto Him. Our successes can be gifts we give to Christ. The Apostle Paul also emphasizes that Timothy hold on to a good conscience and by it he means – no offenses. Keep no offenses. Jesus warns us that if we do not forgive, we cannot be forgiven. Unforgiveness is sin. You must forgive whether or not you feel as though you should. It doesn't mean that the other person was right to be rude to you or whatever the other person said or did; their behavior or words is not ok – but you are forgiving them anyway because you know Christ forgave you when you didn't even know Him. It means that because you are a mature Christian, you forgive. You expect God to bless you. You say with your mouth "I forgive so and so. God, I release the person. You are my rewarder O God." Expect God to bless you and He will. If negative thoughts come, start praying for God to bless the person.

Matthew 6: ¹⁴ For if ye forgive men their trespasses, your heavenly Father will also forgive you:

¹⁵ But if ye forgive not men their trespasses, neither will your Father forgive your trespasses.

Spiritual Gifts can be imparted. That is the gifts God has given to you can be imparted through prayer. It also means that a person's anointing can impact your life so that the anointing comes on your life because of your association with the person. Those who were closest to Jesus received the anointing as well as the authority to preach and teach Christ. Those closest to the Apostles, became leaders of churches. Those who train you in leadership will leave an impression on your life. It is the blessing of God upon you to be associated with people that can build you up, add value to you, strengthen you, bring out the best in you. You should aim to be the same kind of person. You should aim to be someone that can impact others lives so they can excel and honour God living their full potential.

1 Timothy 4:14-15
Neglect not the gift that is in thee, which was given thee by prophecy, with the laying on of the hands of the presbytery.

1. Write a list of your strengths.
   Cover the main aspects of your life include person character traits, education, training, mentors, career, Church involvement, a list of your closest friends that strengthen you, a list of your assets.
2. Write a list of special words God has given you through preachers or prophets or leaders, teachers or mentors. You know they are special words because they directly involve your calling, your potential, your areas of strength or warnings about weaknesses.
3. Create a list of people you can add value to. There should be at least 6 or 7. What can you do to add value to their lives? Pray that you can get opportunities to invest in others. Start doing it. Start getting books to share with others. Start getting teaching or preaching that you can get copies of so you can sow them into others; lives.

4. Create a list of goals for yourself. Be sure to aim for your dreams. What do you want to accomplish within 1 year, 5 years, 10 years etc. Start a plan to begin your 1 year achievements. Start a monthly plan of personal growth. Aim that once a day you will invest in yourself books, cds, podcasts etc. for personal growth.
5. Pray over your lists. Pray for wisdom, discernment. Pray over the people you are mentoring. Pray for others' success.

MAKE THE PROPHETIC YOUR PRIORITY
15 Meditate upon these things give thyself wholly to them that thy profiting may appear to all.

Make it a point to constantly add to your goals. Monthly, yearly etc. The truth is that those who write their goals are approximately 10% or the population. Of those 10% who write their goals, more than 80% achieve them. It is essential that you write your goals, dreams, aspirations etc. It is your chance of succeeding in those areas.

16 take heed unto thyself and unto the doctrine, continue in them, for in doing this thou shalt both save thyself and them that hear thee.

KEEP SOUND DOCTRINE

This is a specific warning about keeping to the truths of the Scriptures. Bible study and Bible reading should be an important aspect of your life. Through it, you build your spirit. You strengthen yourself. You can apply the scriptures to your everyday life. Never go outside the Word of God (The Scriptures). This means living your Christian life each day all the days of your life. Realize God is the source of your success. God has given you the talents. You are His. An important aspect that helps Christians to constantly give glory to God is by honouring Him with our giving. The tithe is not controversial. It is necessary. Giving beyond the tithe is a place of joy beyond what one can imagine. It means you realize you are blessed by God so you can bless others. You give to the gospel. You give to support worthy projects. You are a generous person. You value others so you give so others can be blessed.

Malachi 3: [10] Bring ye all the tithes into the storehouse, that there may be meat in mine house, and prove me now herewith, saith the LORD of hosts, if I will not open you the windows of heaven, and pour you out a blessing, that there shall not be room enough to receive it.

STIR UP THE GIFTS
2 Timothy 1:6
Wherefore I put thee in remembrance that thou stir up the gift of god which is in thee by the putting on of my hands.

Stirring up of your gifts means knowing them first. It also means using them. You can stir your spiritual gifts by praying them. Literally say " I stir the gift of faith" Pray over yourself. Stir yourself. Pray that God will make you a blessing to those you encounter each day. Realize that God can use your words to cheer someone, to impart life to someone. Your giving can make a difference to someone. Your words of encouragement can steer a person's life so he or she is enlightened. Intentionally pray you can add value to someone each day.

DO AND KEEP DOING WHAT IS RIGHT

2 Timothy 3:14
Continue in the things thou hast learned and hast been assured of knowing of whom thou hast learned them.

In long races, there are many who start running like jack rabbits – but there are not so many finishing the long races at that pace. Some don't finish. It is essential that you run consistently. The goal in a race is the finish line. Don't stop running until you go beyond the finish line. Complete your life successfully so there are no regrets. Consistently live for Christ. Consistently keep giving, serving, sowing into others so that your success continues. God promises to bless those that honour His Word (The Scriptures).

PASS IT ON TO THE NEXT ONES
2 Timothy 2:2 the same commit thou to faithful men who shall be able to teach others also.

Keep imparting to others. You should constantly be extending your circle of trainees. Start with giving. Start discipling. Pray for God to use you to build, to add value by your words, your giving, your investments in others. Continue to sow into new people. Train others to train others also. What occurs is explosive growth of a sphere of authority. It can be in your workplace or it can be in your church or your society. It is essential to keep training others to train others. It means the truths you have learned live beyond your life.

Choosing those to mentor

Investing in people in your sphere of authority can be as simple as giving them a present that can encourage them to develop in their areas of strength. It can also mean a discipleship or mentoring or coaching approach as discussed in the previous chapters. God may directly speak to you to give to a person or people or a family, but you should also select people yourself. You should be wise concerning those you invest long term with. You do not just choose anyone to invest in. There must be potential in the person, willingness to learn, success, compatibility, teachability, humility, godly character. Create a list of qualities you believe are essential to a leader. Create a list of those traits you believe you yourself possess. The people you choose can learn from you in those areas.

God raised up a judge in Israel named Gideon. The Israelites were oppressed by the Midianites. They did not have freedom of worship, didn't have ownership of their own land. Gideon gathered an army together as God called him to do. Twenty-two thousand people gathered to fight for their freedom. God spoke to Gideon to thin the ranks. Gideon was to instruct those who were fearful to return and not stay. Next he brought the people to the water. Those who lapped water as a dog with his tongue would be chosen. Of those who were gathered only 300 remained. It was a way of showing that the God of Israel could use the 300 to defeat the army of the Melanites rather than for Israel to believe they defeated the army without God. This does not mean you cannot choose many people but it means you should be discerning. You should not intrust your life investments to just anyone.

You don't choose just anyone – Gideons 300

Judges 7: ² And the LORD said unto Gideon, The people that are with thee are too many for me to give the Midianites into their hands, lest Israel vaunt themselves against me, saying, Mine own hand hath saved me.

³ Now therefore go to, proclaim in the ears of the people, saying, Whosoever is fearful and afraid, let him return and depart early from mount Gilead. And there returned of the people twenty and two thousand; and there remained ten thousand.

⁴ And the LORD said unto Gideon, The people are yet too many; bring them down unto the water, and I will try them for thee there: and it shall be, that of whom I say unto thee, This shall go with thee, the same shall go with thee; and of whomsoever I say unto thee, This shall not go with thee, the same shall not go.

⁵ So he brought down the people unto the water: and the LORD said unto Gideon, Every one that lappeth of the water with his tongue, as a dog lappeth, him shalt thou set by himself; likewise every one that boweth down upon his knees to drink.

⁶ And the number of them that lapped, putting their hand to their mouth, were three hundred men: but all the rest of the people bowed down upon their knees to drink water.

⁷ And the LORD said unto Gideon, By the three hundred men that lapped will I save you, and deliver the Midianites into thine hand: and let all the other people go every man unto his place.

Those you choose to invest in with your life, your resources, your wisdom etc. must be worthy of the choosing. Pray for the gift of discerning of spirits. Pray that God will give you wisdom Choosing people to invest in. There may be some you start with that you release from your sphere. Should there be a resistance or refusal to change in an area of weakness, a moral issue unresolved or some hindrance of the person's own choosing – an issue of will – the person will not grow beyond the point he or she is in, you should not continue with the person anymore.

Matthew 7: 6 Cast not your pearls before swine, lest they trample them under their feet, and turn again and rend you.

Should the occasion arise that you dismiss someone from mentoring, do not let it stop you from choosing others. As a teacher my aim is student success. I want the students to obtain an A. I will in no way give them, marks they don't earn. I provide support, am flexible, generous etc. but there are some who fail because they do not choose to use the assistance or guidance. Although my aim is that all would succeed, not all do because of their own choosing. So it is with mentorship. Invest by speaking with the person, discussing success, areas of weakness or strength, his or her goals or dreams and their list of steps to achieve them. God will use your discernment and your strengths to select books to recommend or give them. Their may be Cd's or conferences you sponsor the person to get. It means giving to the person as though you would invest in yourself.

Discuss the materials with the person. Ask questions that cause them to consider their present course and how it can improve. Invest in them as you are training a cherished daughter or son. You give not expecting to receive something except the other person's growth. As they grow spiritually, as well as professionally, they will begin to give to you in some way. Their success is accomplished when you see them training others. The relationship begins with a mostly one sided giving, but matures into synergy as you provide opportunities for the person to succeed. You may include them in your ministry at Church or in your workplace. It means trusting them with opportunities to succeed.

Godly character is essential. If the person is not living a godly life, you can not expect the person to keep godly principles in the workplace or in the ministry. The criteria discussed as points of choosing leaders in the church should be criteria we prayerfully consider when choosing those who we will let in our inner circle and sow our lives into.

1 Timothy 3: 1 This is a true saying, if a man desire the office of a bishop, he desireth a good work.

Someone who wants to improve is someone worth choosing. Someone who knows you are experienced and trusts you to speak into his or her life is worth investing in.

2 A bishop then must be blameless, the husband of one wife, vigilant, sober, of good behaviour, given to hospitality, apt to teach;

Morally the person should be living a life without reproach. Christian leaders are known by the lives they lead not simply the words they speak. The words as well as the lifestyle must be consistent for a Christian leader.

3 Not given to wine, no striker, not greedy of filthy lucre; but patient, not a brawler, not covetous;

The person must value his or her family as a gift from God. If the person is divided in his or her closest relationships, he or she cannot learn from you how to establish deep connecting meaningful relationship with others in mentoring relationships.

4 One that ruleth well his own house, having his children in subjection with all gravity;

5 (For if a man know not how to rule his own house, how shall he take care of the church of God?)

Entrust authority wisely. Discern the potential, the maturity and the spiritual aspects of the person you are investing in. The person must show some personal achievements – some self-discipline, desire to achieve dreams beyond himself or herself.

6 Not a novice, lest being lifted up with pride he fall into the condemnation of the devil.

7 Moreover he must have a good report of them which are without; lest he fall into reproach and the snare of the devil.

8 Likewise must the deacons be grave, not double tongued, not given to much wine, not greedy of filthy lucre;

9 Holding the mystery of the faith in a pure conscience.

10 And let these also first be proved; then let them use the office of a deacon, being found blameless.

The Words a person speaks should align with Scripture. The person should not be speaking words that are negative or condemning of himself or others. Negative people must first learn to focus on others not themselves. They must become Word of God readers, studiers etc. before they can live the scriptures. The words we speak are containers for life or death.

Proverbs 18: **21** Death and life are in the power of the tongue: and they that love it shall eat the fruit thereof.

Our words should build up, strengthen, encourage, add value to others. We should know the words we speak and own them. That means we don't say negative things about people. We do not judge others with our words. We do not slander others. These are as knives that can hurt others. Our words should bless, impart a blessing. We can encourage others with our words. We cannot just say anything. Living in the Spirit means letting God's Word be final authority over every area of our lives.

11 Even so must their wives be grave, not slanderers, sober, faithful in all things.

Psalms 19: ¹⁴ Let the words of my mouth, and the meditation of my heart, be acceptable in thy sight, O LORD, my strength, and my redeemer.

The moral condition of his or her life is an indication of his or her strengths or weaknesses. Please realize I am speaking of training leaders for Christian ministry. The criteria are strict. My own criteria would be strict, but God's established criteria is the standard. If the person resists any aspect of the Christian faith or doctrine, he or she cannot be promoted. The core beliefs of the Christian faith are in the Scriptures. Our lives must reflect our beliefs in the Scriptures. Someone entrusted in your inner circle cannot be someone without the same core values.

¹² Let the deacons be the husbands of one wife, ruling their children and their own houses well.

¹³ For they that have used the office of a deacon well purchase to themselves a good degree, and great boldness in the faith which is in Christ Jesus.

2 Corinthians 6: ¹⁴ Be ye not unequally yoked together with unbelievers: for what fellowship hath righteousness with unrighteousness? and what communion hath light with darkness?

Should you have become mentored by a Christian sowing into your life, you will understand the bond I am speaking of. It is a mentor/student relationship. At least it begins that way. You can connect because your core values are the same. Your belief system is the same. Should someone desire a promotion in Christian ministry or as a Christian in his or her workplace, Christ must be the center of his or her life. Godly character means spiritual fruit evident in his or her words, life choices, decision making etc.

Galatians 5: [22] But the fruit of the Spirit is love, joy, peace, longsuffering, gentleness, goodness, faith,

[23] Meekness, temperance: against such there is no law.

1. Prayerfully consider those you believe you can impact or mentor.
2. Start with an informal get together – a sharing of resources, speaking. There should be an invitation to mentorship or your life investing in others.
3. The person should agree, be honest, trustworthy, excellent. There should be gratitude. The person should know it is important to his or her development.
4. Pray for wisdom for yourself – for those you mentor.

James 3: [17] But the wisdom that is from above is first pure, then peaceable, gentle, and easy to be intreated, full of mercy and good fruits, without partiality, and without hypocrisy.

In your decision making, there should be peace. If there is not, it means that the decision should change. It could mean prayer for an answer. It could mean postponing a decision. It could mean not making changes. The Holy Spirit's presence comes as we make life investments in others.

Chapter end questions

1. What are major decisions you've made? List 2-3 explain how you made the decisions as well as the results.
2. Are you in a place of decision at present? What are your choices? Make a list of positive aspects should you choose it. Make list of negative aspects if you choose it. Is there some Interesting aspect to choosing it that is unique, special, worth pursuing? Discuss these results with your mentors, closest friends, those who you can trust with your dreams.
3. How can you create a meaningful mentorship relationship? Plan some special conversation to sow into someone's life. Invest in some excellent books to assist you in your mentorship. Invest in some special books, cd's or other materials that you can get for those you are mentoring. Be sure to schedule a follow up discussion.

Conclusion

Throughout the chapters of this book, I 've lead you through scriptures concerning the preparation for ministry and career success as a Christian of excellent spirit, the calling, the training or mentoring and using your gifts, talents and success to train others in ministry.

There has been emphasis on life choices to be considered for ministry/career success. Rather than emphasize career or ministry, I've discussed the mature Christian as both career and ministry. The calling of a Christian is a lifelong calling. It is necessary that each Christian be involved in the Church serving in some way. Some may be youth pastors or Sunday school teachers.

Those called to the five-fold ministry should be constantly involved in evangelism and missions in some way also. The main emphasis has been "equipping the saints" for the work of the ministry. The Church must use her spiritual gifts to effectively witness Christ in the earth. The Church body is necessary – not just the ministry team. All Christians are called to follow Christ. All Christians are to reproduce themselves by making disciples.

In closing comments for you to consider are the following points.

God wants us to pray for labourers – it is Jesus' prayer request. It can begin with you. Say yes to God - preaching, teaching, serving etc. Encourage others to serve Christ also. Each member of the Body of Christ is important and should offer himself/herself to God wholly so that God can use you. Start praying for a release of labourers for God's kingdom. Be a willing vessel. Should the Holy Spirit prompt you to serve, give or encourage – don't hesitate to do it. Offer yourself as a sacrifice, and expect God to use you each day of your life.

John 4: [35] Say not ye, There are yet four months, and then cometh harvest? behold, I say unto you, Lift up your eyes, and look on the fields; for they are white already to harvest.

[36] And he that reapeth receiveth wages, and gathereth fruit unto life eternal: that both he that soweth and he that reapeth may rejoice together.

[37] And herein is that saying true, One soweth, and another reapeth.

Pray that God will give you compassion for others that moves you in prayer, in stirring up your spiritual gifts and taking action by using the spiritual gifts God has given you to do the works of Christ in the earth. Commit to be a labourer for Christ. It May mean you speak to those you haven't met encouraging them with words God quickens to you. It could be giving to those who can never repay you. It could mean sacrificing entertainment for prayer or more Bible reading. What it means is you have committed your life wholly to Christ. You are on assignment 365 days a year.

Luke 10: [2] Therefore said he unto them, The harvest truly is great, but the labourers are few: pray ye therefore the Lord of the harvest, that he would send forth labourers into his harvest.

Matthew 9: [36] But when he saw the multitudes, he was moved with compassion on them, because they fainted, and were scattered abroad, as sheep having no shepherd.

[37] Then saith he unto his disciples, The harvest truly is plenteous, but the labourers are few;

[38] Pray ye therefore the Lord of the harvest, that he will send forth labourers into his harvest.

As you get experience in ministry, success in ministry and or career, start training others. Start giving to those around you. Get others involved in opportunities to serve or give or minister with you. The more people you get involved in living life for a higher reason than self – is your success. There will be some you will especially sow into. They will be those you mentor or disciple. Pray for discernment so you will know who to disciple, who to sow into. Start mentoring others in the things you have succeeded in. Release people by encouraging them to use their gifts and talents for God.

There are people in destiny decision making positions –
ordinary/ extraordinary – God wants you to serve him – He has
need of you. This Releases you into a destiny beyond what you
can imagine. You should also speak life into those you perceive
desire to excel in their Christian lives – service for Christ as
leaders. Your decision to live radically for Christ, is a decision to
train others for serving: in the Church, in the community, in the
workplace. God is able to do exceedingly abundantly above and
beyond what you can ask (Ephesians 3: 20)

Ephesians 3: **20** Now unto him that is able to do
exceeding abundantly above all that we ask or think,
according to the power that worketh in us,

God wants you to know there is an extraordinary way - a
higher way – the way of Spirit – the Way of God's Word. The Holy
Spirit is the most awesome life coach. As he prompts you, obey.
Aim for excellence with your life. Keep aiming for excellence until
Christ receives you from this earthly life. Your target is to live life
on earth as though you are living each day for Christ only – do it
with passion. Do it with excellence. Others will be attracted to you
because of it.

Philippians 3: **14** I press toward the mark for the prize of
the high calling of God in Christ Jesus.

Special Words of Encouragement

Hold onto those special prophetic words you've received. Pray over the special words of encouragement you've received – write them. Read them Pray them. Respect the Christians who have imparted into your life. Honour them. Bless them. Live your life to be a blessing, serving Christ by valuing people. Add value to people by encouraging words, sowing Cd's books etc. into their lives. Live life giving, serving, encouraging – you are blessed to be a blessing to others.

Pray over yourself the fruit of Spirit. Pray that all of the fruit of the Spirit will be in you that you may be Christlike. Remember living your life in Christ – you are seated in Christ in heavenly places with Christ Jesus. He raised you up to sit with Him. We are in Christ. Christ is sitting on the Throne of glory. Christ in you the hope of glory.

Ephesians 2: **20** Which he wrought in Christ, when he raised him from the dead, and set him at his own right hand in the heavenly places,

21 Far above all principality, and power, and might, and dominion, and every name that is named, not only in this world, but also in that which is to come:

22 And hath put all things under his feet, and gave him to be the head over all things to the church,

23 Which is his body, the fulness of him that filleth all in all.

Ephesians 2: **5** Even when we were dead in sins, hath quickened us together with Christ, (by grace ye are saved;)

6 And hath raised us up together, and made us sit together in heavenly places in Christ Jesus:

Seated with Christ means you are in the risen Body of Christ. All authority has been given to the Church to witness for Christ, to preach, teach minister, salvation, healing, deliverance, prosperity - the kingdom of God. Live the Word of God. Do not depart from the Word of God. Pray the Word be engrafted into your soul. The way of the Word – Spirit never contradicts the Word. As you are living scripturally, the Word is shinning in you and through you. It is preaching Christ by living Christ. Others will notice the difference and want to know why you are excelling in so many areas of your life. They will desire to know the God you serve.

Importance of the Word of God – God's Word is the highest authority for all decision making. Apply the Word in your daily as well as destiny decisions.

2 Timothy 3: **16** All scripture is given by inspiration of God, and is profitable for doctrine, for reproof, for correction, for instruction in righteousness:

17 That the man of God may be perfect, thoroughly furnished unto all good works.

God's word is settled in heaven. God's Word is inerrant, inspired by the Holy Spirit, meaning it cannot change. It is God's will for humans. It is a manual for life on earth. All topics that could be studied on earth are covered in it. Jesus in you is evident with your life aligning with God's Word.

Psalm 119: [89] For ever, O LORD, thy word is settled in heaven.

Colossians 1: [27] To whom God would make known what is the riches of the glory of this mystery among the Gentiles; which is Christ in you, the hope of glory:

Jesus the highest name by which men might be saved – He set his Word above his name. The Word of God is sure. The Word of God is right. The Word of God is truth.

Philippians 2: [9] Wherefore God also hath highly exalted him, and given him a name which is above every name:

Psalm 138: [2] I will worship toward thy holy temple, and praise thy name for thy lovingkindness and for thy truth: for thou hast magnified thy word above all thy name.

Jesus is the living Word of God.

John 1: 1 The word is God. Christ is living in you in the person of the Holy Spirit. Pray that your life can align with God's Word.

John 1:1 In the beginning was the Word, and the Word was with God, and the Word was God.

The engrafted Word saves your soul. As a gardener, I've engrafted some trees and shrubs. It means taking part of a living plant and attaching it to the body of a different living plant. You make deep cuts in the shrub or tree you will implant in. You place the grafted branch or part and seal it together. The two grow together as one. There is a total joining, so it is one. The Word of God should be in your hearts so that we align with it totally.

James 1: **21** Wherefore lay apart all filthiness and superfluity of naughtiness, and receive with meekness the engrafted word, which is able to save your souls.

You are becoming a living epistle. The more of God's Word you get inside of you, the more your life aligns with God's Word. Pray that you may desire God's Word more than silver or gold. The Word of God you live may be the only Word of God some people encounter.

Philippians 2: **2** Ye are our epistle written in our hearts, known and read of all men:

3 Forasmuch as ye are manifestly declared to be the epistle of Christ ministered by us, written not with ink, but with the Spirit of the living God; not in tables of stone, but in fleshy tables of the heart.

He will write his words in our hearts; we will be his people; he will be our God. It is God's promise for Israel. It is His promise for His covenant people. By faith in Jesus Christ, we inherit the blessings of Abraham and the Mosaic covenant.

Jeremiah 31: [33] But this shall be the covenant that I will make with the house of Israel; After those days, saith the LORD, I will put my law in their inward parts, and write it in their hearts; and will be their God, and they shall be my people.

Some people cannot recognize the extraordinary way unless you go get them as Barnabas sought after Saul and got him involved in ministry. They must be released or invited. Pray for discernment so you can build up the body of Christ by encouraging others to use their gifts and talents. As sure as a spark is necessary to light a candle, it is necessary that you spark others with encouragement to use their gifts and talents.

Acts 9: [27] But Barnabas took him, and brought him to the apostles, and declared unto them how he had seen the Lord in the way, and that he had spoken to him, and how he had preached boldly at Damascus in the name of Jesus.

Paul and Barnabus

Acts 11: [25] Then departed Barnabas to Tarsus, for to seek Saul:

[26] And when he had found him, he brought him unto Antioch. And it came to pass, that a whole year they assembled themselves

with the church, and taught much people. And the disciples were called Christians first in Antioch.

Destiny Decisions impact our earthly lives as well as our spheres of authority. One decision leads to a series of choices. Each choice leads to a different pathway of choices. It is necessary that Christians prayerfully consider each major decision in life. It is essential Christians be lead by the Holy Spirit, the Word of God and wise counsel.

There are some seasoned ministers apostles, prophets, pastors, teachers evangelists who should be training other leaders. Should you be successful in ministry – you should be training others. There are some servants, givers, encouragers, mercies that should training up others in the body of Christ. It is necessary for leaders to train leaders, but it is also necessary for servants to train other servants. The human body reproducing cells daily is necessary for life; so is the Body of Christ-we must keep reproducing in all aspects of it: encouragers, givers, servants, mercies.

The Bible model is apprenticeship with the elders teaching candidates. It is essential to train others, who will teach others etc.

2 Timothy: [2] And the things that thou hast heard of me among many witnesses, the same commit thou to faithful men, who shall be able to teach others also.

You can impart the things you've learned so that the body of Christ can be built up, strengthened, equipped for the work of the ministry. Pray that you can impart a legacy to others that will outlive you. Pray that it is Christ, the things of Christ you impart. The purpose for each member of the Body of Christ is that we sow into others. We are evangelizing, doing missions, sowing into the Church, strengthening the body, living life in the Spirit.

Ephesians 4: [12] For the perfecting of the saints, for the work of the ministry, for the edifying of the body of Christ:

[13] Till we all come in the unity of the faith, and of the knowledge of the Son of God, unto a perfect man, unto the measure of the stature of the fulness of Christ:

Invest in others lives – as someone invested in you – what people do you credit for teaching you the things of CHRIST? You've got opportunity to invest in others – who will invest in others. Start giving. Start connecting. Start serving. Start mentoring. Live your life to equip others, to add value to others.

Chapter end questions
1. List the people who first mentored you in Christ. What did they do?
2. List the people who first mentored you towards your career choice. What did they do?
3. List the people who mentored you in your career choice. What did they do?
4. List the people you are mentoring. In what ways are you impacting them?

5. List the mentors in your life presently. Explain how they are encouraging you to obtain your goals.

PRAYERS

PRAYERS The following prayers are samples of prayers you could pray for important reasons. You could pray using your own words. The prayers are meant as examples only.

PRAYER FOR SALVATION Thank you- Jesus that you died for me on the cross. Thank you that you rose from the dead and ascended into heaven. Thank you that you are coming back again. I thank you Jesus for forgiving my sins. Thank you for your blood that cleanses me from all sin and unrighteousness. Thank you that your blood makes me holy. Thank you for saving me. Fill me with the Holy Spirit to overflowing. I pray for the baptism of the Holy Spirit. Lead me to other people who love you and serve you and that can help me know more about you. Give me the discerning of spirits strong. I thank you and praise you. With my mouth, I confess Jesus Christ is my LORD. Amen.

PRAYER FOR BAPTISM OF THE HOLY SPIRIT Thank you- Jesus that you promised to send the gift of the Holy Spirit to us. Thank you that this promise is to all believers. I am a believer. I want all of you that you will give me. I want to know you God. Baptize me in the Holy Spirit with the evidence of speaking in other tongues. I believe you want to fill me to overflowing with your Spirit so that I might be an effective witness for Christ on the earth. Thank you for saving me. Thank you for your Holy presence. [begin praising God for what He has done for you – sing worship choruses and praise God in your natural language. Believe that He is present with you – start praising and worshipping Him. As phrases come to you in other tongues, say them – praise God with new tongues.] I praise you. I thank you. I receive the baptism of the Holy Spirit.

PRAYER FOR RELEASING ANGELS   God, I thank you that angels are ministering spirits sent as ministers to us. I pray over my prayer request NAME IT HERE. God I pray release angels to perform it. I thank you for releasing the answer to me. I praise you for it. Amen.

PRAYER FOR RESISTING EVIL   I am the redeemed of the LORD. Jesus Christ has saved me. I am a new creation in Christ Jesus. Jesus blood covers me. I live in the spirit. The Holy Spirit of God fills my spirit. O Holy Spirit quicken me; give me wisdom. Pray [expecting God will give you discerning of spirits so you will have the right words to speak.]   In the name of Jesus Christ, I bind you. I rebuke you evil spirit. In the name of Jesus, I command you to go out. You have no place in my life. I cast you out. You have no place with me. I am covered by the blood of Jesus and His righteousness is my righteousness. Go out evil spirit in the name of Jesus

Christ! Thank you, Holy Spirit for your holy presence.
Release angels to drive out the enemy. Thank you.
Amen.

PRAYER FOR PROTECTION   Holy Spirit release angels to
protect me. I plead the blood of Jesus over me. I pray
the protection you promise to your people. Cover me
Jesus. Holy Spirit give me wisdom, discernment and
understanding. Thank you for angels that guard over me.
Thank you for your blood that protects me and a hedge
of protection around me. I praise you O God. [praise
God with some worship choruses and expect God's holy
presence to be manifest in you]. Thank you. O God for
protection.

PRAYER FOR HEALING

Lord Jesus, thank you that you gave your life for me so
that I can be saved, healed and delivered. I thank you for
the scripture that by your stripes I am healed. I thank
you for my healing.   NAME THE DISEASE I bind you in
the name of Jesus. I cast you out. I pray over myself that
I would be whole spirit, soul and body.   Thank you,
God. for your healing manifestation in my life. I give you
all the glory. Amen.   PRAYER OF REPENTENCE   Jesus,
thank you for your blood shed for me. I repent of the sin
of NAME IT. I thank you for liberty from sin. I cut off the
root of iniquity in my family. I thank you for your
empowering presence to live a Holy life. Holy Spirit lead

and guide me in the paths of righteousness. Thank you for giving me godly desires. Let my life align with your word. In Jesus name. Amen.   Prayer of dedication as a giver   God, thank you for prospering me. Let me be a giver you can use to give to others. God let my character be humble and giving so that you place things and wealth in my hands, and I will give as you lead me. If you prosper me with more than enough, I will obey your promptings to give to the gospel, to people and for the glory of God. Use me as a giver. I give myself wholly to you. In Jesus name. Amen.

Prayer for Israel

God I pray for the peace of Jerusalem (Psalm 122: 6). I pray for all of Israel to be saved (Romans 11: 25). I pray for you to make Jerusalem a praise and a fame throughout all the earth. (Isaiah 62:7). I pray you will keep Israel as the apple of your eye and hide her under the shadow of your wing. (Psalm 17:8). I pray for the Word of God to be written in their hearts. (Jeremiah 31: 33; Ezekiel 11: 19) Reveal yourself as Jesus the Messiah to the people of Israel and Jewish people everywhere. Amen.

Of course, you can pray other things for the blessing of Israel. It is essential to pray scripture as God has made covenant with Israel.

PRAYER OF CONCESCRATION

I offer myself to you a living sacrifice which is my reasonable service. I give myself wholly – spirit soul body. Holy Spirit lead me, direct me, guide me in all areas of my life. I submit myself to you Holy Spirit. Let my mouth speak words of life. Let me encourage, exhort, comfort. Let me add value to those in my life. Let me magnify Christ with my life each day, all my life. Amen.

PRAYER FOR A MENTOR

O God, I pray, let a Godly Christian mentor come into my life. Bring me into supernatural favour with those who can train and equip me. Give me wisdom, discernment. I pray for a release of a mentor as you released Elijah to train Elisha, as you released The Apostle Paul to train Timothy. Amen.

PRAYER FOR DIVINE CONNECTIONS

O God, I pray for Divine connections. Bring individuals into my life that I can be a blessing to, that I can receive from. I know I must give what I've been given. It's my desire to learn from those who know you, who serve you. It is my desire to bring your encouragement to others. Let there be supernatural favour on my life. As I give, let it be given unto me good measure, pressed down, shaken together and running over. You are the reason I desire to connect with people. Let me give you glory with my life connections. Amen.

PRAYER FOR SUPERNATURAL FAVOUR

God I thank you that the blessings of Abraham are mine by faith. Thank you for the blessings of the Mosaic Covenant. The blessing of God is on my life. I receive supernatural favour with all kinds of individuals: in church, in school, in my career, in society. Use me to bless, encourage, build up others. Let me be a vessel you can use to bless others. Amen.

OTHER BOOKS BY CHRIS LEGEBOW

Available on Amazon.ca Amazon.com or Kindle
Living Word Publishers

Angels: Ministering Spirits
The Christian Charismatic Church
Discipling the Generation
An Excellent Spirit:
Living Life Wholly Unto God
Covenant With God: God's Relationship With Man
Discovering and Using your Spiritual Gifts
Discipling The Generation
Divine Healing in the Scriptures: God's Mercy Towards Man
Israel Our Christian Heritage: Israel Our Christian Destiny
Jesus Christ: Saviour, Healer, Deliverer, LORD
Kinds of Giving: From the Holy Scriptures
Signs of Jesus Coming

Spheres of Authority: Know yours
The Commandments
The Doctrine of Christ: Essential Truths of Scripture
The Five-Fold Ministry: Gifts to the Church
Kinds of Prayer. Knowing Them and Using Them Effectively
Living Life Fully: Knowing your Purpose
The Altar: In the Charismatic Christian Church
The Anointing: The Glory of God
The Charismatic Christian Church
The High Calling: Life Worth Living
The High Life: Communion with the Holy Spirit
The Sacraments: A Charismatic Guide

ABOUT THE AUTHOR

Chris Legebow is a Christian Professor of English and Communications. She has taught at the elementary, high school and College and University levels. She has ministered in her local churches in intercessory prayer, teaching Sunday school and other Christian Doctrine classes to children and youth. She has preached to congregations and given her testimony. Although she was not raised in a Christian home, she came to know Jesus Christ as her Saviour and LORD while she was studying in University. This radically transformed her life in terms of priorities and commitment.

She has a strong passion for the great commission – that Jesus Christ would be preached throughout all the earth believing that it a major sign of the LORD's return. She has been a part of several different types of full gospel charismatic churches but has also gained much of her insight and enlightenment from Christian Media and broadcasting. She hopes to continue ministering, serving, interceding and giving and teaching until the LORD returns

www.ingramcontent.com/pod-product-compliance
Lightning Source LLC
Chambersburg PA
CBHW032035040426
42449CB00007B/901